175
natural sugar
desserts

Angelina and Ari Dayan

Robert
ROSE

175 Natural Sugar Desserts
Copyright © 2007, 2009 Les Éditions de l'Homme, a division of Groupe Sogides Inc.,
subsidiary of Groupe Livre Quebecor Média Inc. (Montreal, Quebec)
Cover and text design copyright © 2009 Robert Rose Inc.

A portion of this book was previously published in French under the title *Les Desserts sans sucre ajouté* (Les Éditions de l'Homme, 2007).

For complete cataloguing information, see page 216.

The recipes in this book have been carefully tested by our kitchen and our tasters. To the best of our knowledge, they are safe and nutritious for ordinary use and users. For those people with food or other allergies, or who have special food requirements or health issues, please read the suggested contents of each recipe carefully and determine whether or not they may create a problem for you. All recipes are used at the risk of the consumer.

We cannot be responsible for any hazards, loss or damage that may occur as a result of any recipe use.

For those with special needs, allergies, requirements or health problems, in the event of any doubt, please contact your medical adviser prior to the use of any recipe.

Editors: Jennifer MacKenzie and Sue Sumeraj
Proofreader: Sheila Wawanash
Indexer: Gillian Watts
Design and Production: Joseph Gisini/PageWave Graphics Inc.
Photography: Tango
Food Styling: Jacques Faucher
Prop Styling: Luce Meunier

Cover image: Mascarpone Fruitcake (page 120)

We acknowledge the financial support of the Government of Canada through the Book Publishing Industry Development Program (BPIDP) for our publishing activities.

Published by Robert Rose Inc.
120 Eglinton Avenue East, Suite 800, Toronto, Ontario, Canada M4P 1E2
Tel: (416) 322-6552   Fax: (416) 322-6936

Printed and bound in Canada

1 2 3 4 5 6 7 8 9   CPL   17 16 15 14 13 12 11 10 09

Contents

Author's Note

• •

I wrote this book with my son Ari. He is notably the author of the chapter "Why Natural Sugar Desserts?" and is the one who came up with the general idea for the book. I created the recipes and wrote their introductions with the help of my nine cats, who actively participated, if only by making a mess in the kitchen and by trying to taste everything they could get their paws on. Many recipes are named after them, so you'll find their names scattered throughout the book: Chloe, Vicky, Vlad, Maxi, Little Prince, Princess Valy and so on. If you would like to meet them, or if you have any questions about the recipes, please visit my website, www.angelinadayan.com.

— Angelina Dayan

*The authors would like to thank Jennifer and Sue
for their excellent editing.*

Why Natural Sugar Desserts?

This book is for all health-conscious people who enjoy homemade desserts and baked goods. If you are trying to reduce your intake of sugar, or eliminate it completely, our delicious recipes will let you continue to enjoy wonderful desserts. And you'll be able to offer your children something other than cavity-producing sweets and sugary baked goods!

Just because a dessert has no refined sugar doesn't mean it has no flavor. On the contrary, you'll be able to taste the true flavor of the ingredients, as sugar tends to mask them. If you've ordered an apple pie in a restaurant, it likely had more sugar than apples! In our recipes, we don't use white or brown sugar or artificial sweeteners. Instead, our desserts are sweetened either with naturally sweet fruit or with natural sugars. People who have tasted our desserts have enjoyed them all and were surprised to learn that they didn't contain any refined sugar.

The Dangers of Sugar

Sugar is a relatively recent food, in that it became popular only in the 20th century. Before that, it was considered to be more a spice than a food in its own right. The main problem is that sugar does not exist naturally: it is produced by refining another food, such as sugarcane or sugar beets. It is very easy to consume too much sugar (and too often) for our bodies to handle. It's actually much harder to consume large amounts of carbohydrates when we eat whole foods, such as fruit and whole grains, because we fill up more quickly.

Let's look at what happens in the body when we consume sugar. Since the refined product is stripped from the fiber in fruit, it passes directly (and therefore too quickly) into the bloodstream without being digested. The level of glucose in the blood, which should stay close to 1 gram per liter, quickly rises to above normal levels. As a result, the pancreas secretes an excessive amount of insulin to lower the level of sugar in the blood. The result is postprandial hypoglycemia, in which we experience symptoms such as nervousness, cold sweat, tremors, fatigue, yawning, hunger and the well-known feeling of being downright drained. So what do we do to circumvent these symptoms? We eat more sugar! And we become dependent on it.

A growing number of people in Western society now suffer from obesity and other weight-related problems; in addition, recent studies show that sugar plays a role in various diseases, such as diabetes and heart disease. That is why it is important to limit our sugar consumption and free ourselves from our dependence on sugary foods. One day, we may well find out that sugar, when misused (which is, unfortunately, very often), can be just as harmful as cigarettes or excessive use of alcohol. There may come a time when foods that contain a lot of sugar will have their own warning label, saying something like "Consuming large amounts of sugar can be detrimental to your health."

People often think that sugar is part of a balanced diet and that we can't exclude it because "we need it" or "it's a source of energy." This isn't true — we can easily go through life without ever eating it. We certainly managed fine before the process for refining sugar was discovered. The human body *does* need carbohydrates, but we can easily find them in natural whole foods, such as fruit, cereals, grains, legumes and so on.

A Natural Diet Is the Key to Well-Being

Everything we eat has a direct effect on our bodies and thus on our overall long-term health. It is therefore best to consume foods that are as natural as possible, with the least amount of processing. As a general rule, foods lose much of their nutritional value as they go through the various stages of processing, and many other, less natural ingredients are often added. Some disturbing studies show a link between these additives and an increased risk of developing certain diseases, but this doesn't prevent the food-processing industry from using them.

Don't despair: you can still eat well and enjoy food; you just have to be more careful about what you buy. Keep this in mind when you shop for ingredients to prepare the recipes in this book. If you choose to buy ready-made dough, for example, select the most natural product possible, made without hydrogenated fats.

Desserts and Dieting

Even though our desserts are free of refined sugar and, for the most part, have far fewer calories than traditional desserts, it is still important to follow certain basic principals if you are watching your weight. As with anything, moderation is the key! Instead of finishing every meal on a sweet note or having a sweet snack to satisfy a sudden hunger pang, save desserts for special occasions, or at most a few times a week. Your scale will thank you, and you will feel healthier when you're not overloading your body with carbohydrates. In addition, you'll enjoy desserts that much more, because they'll really be a treat, rather than a habit.

We hope you enjoy our desserts as much as we've enjoyed writing this book. We would be happy to respond to any of your comments or suggestions. If you have questions about our recipes or products specified in this book, visit our website: www.angelinadayan.com.

Shopping for Ingredients

Natural Sugars

It may not be necessary to add a sweetener to your dessert if you're using fruit that is naturally very sweet. If, however, you need a sweetener, use a natural sugar: agave syrup, stevia or xylitol. If you can't find any of these, you can use honey. For some traditional recipes, we've used maple syrup, but you can substitute agave syrup, which is slightly sweeter and has a lower glycemic index.

Agave Syrup

Agave syrup is a natural sweetener with a very low glycemic index. It is made by concentrating the juice from the heart of the blue agave plant, a type of cactus native to Mexico (and the same plant used in the production of tequila). This nectar, known as "honey water" in Mexico, is similar to honey in flavor and color and has a high fructose content. How sweet it is varies from brand to brand, depending on the concentration. In our recipes, we used Organic Raw Blue Agave Nectar, which is about one and a quarter times sweeter than refined sugar. You can find it at health food stores, specialty food stores and some major supermarkets with a natural foods section, as well as online.

Xylitol

Xylitol is a natural sweetener found in plums, among other fruits. It contains 40% fewer carbohydrates than sugar and is absorbed more slowly into the body. Seven teaspoons (35 mL) of xylitol affect glucose levels as much as a single teaspoon (5 mL) of refined sugar! Yet its sweetening power is the same as that of sugar and, unlike artificial sweeteners, it has no unpleasant taste. Note that it cannot be used with brewer's yeast, but it does work well with baking powder. You can find it at health food stores, specialty food stores and some major supermarkets with a natural foods section, as well as online.

Honey

Honey is produced by bees and is derived from plants. Due to its high carbohydrate content, it should be used only in small quantities. It has roughly one and a quarter times the sweetening power of sugar. In particular, we use:

- Heather blossom honey, which is dark in color and rather thick. It works well in cakes and cookies.
- Lime blossom honey, which adds a wonderful aroma to desserts.
- Acacia honey to sweeten yogurt and ice cream.
- Buckwheat honey, a robust, dark honey produced in Canada. It is best used to sweeten savory foods or when a strong flavor is desired.

Maple Syrup

Primarily a product of eastern Canada and the northeastern United States, maple syrup is made from the sap of maple trees. We drizzle it over pancakes and crêpes, and use it to sweeten some desserts, sorbets and ice cream. It should be used sparingly, as it is high in carbohydrates.

Stevia

Stevia rebaudiana is a perennial aster-like tropical plant native to Paraguay. Stevia has incredible sweetening power and an extremely low glycemic index (practically zero). It has also been shown in many recent studies to have excellent health benefits. It is widely used in Japan, the United States, Germany and (for centuries) Paraguay, and is cultivated in China on a large scale.

Stevia can be used in its natural state, simply by grinding the dried leaves into powder. It is also available as fresh stevia leaves and dried herbal powder (which is green). These are about 3 to 4 times sweeter than table sugar. The refined extracts of stevia, called steviosides, are 200 to 300 times sweeter than granulated sugar. Powdered stevia extract is 85% to 95% steviosides.

If stevia is available as a sweetener in your area, and you plan to substitute it for the natural sugar called for in these recipes, we recommend using powdered stevia extract. In general, you'll use 1½ tsp (7 mL) powdered stevia extract in place of 1 cup (250 mL) granulated sugar. Because you need considerably less powdered stevia extract than other natural sugars, most recipes require the addition of more liquid as well, to balance the ratio of liquid to dry ingredients. Where stevia will work in a recipe, we've provided a tip that explains how to substitute it. There are also stevia blends available, often labeled "for baking," that contain steviosides and other ingredients. But note that different brands of powdered stevia extract and stevia blends vary in sweetness, so it's best to check the instructions on the package to determine the quantity to use.

In North America, you can find stevia in health food stores, specialty food stores and some major supermarkets with a natural foods section, as well as online. Depending on the government regulations in your area, stevia products may not be labeled as sweeteners; rather, they may be labeled and sold as food supplements or as dietary supplements or as a dietary ingredient of a dietary supplement. While stevia is widely available in the United States and Canada, it is not currently approved for use as a sweetener in the European Union, and cannot be purchased in the United Kingdom. Readers who live in Europe are advised to use one of the natural sugars suggested in the ingredients list for the recipe.

Fresh Fruit

We buy fruit daily to prevent it from drying out and losing vitamins. Always select ripe, high-quality, sweet fruit varieties.

- *Apples:* Many new apple varieties have become available in the last few years. Red-skinned apples, such as Fuji, Jazz, Pink Lady or Elstar, have the sweetest flavor. We primarily use Jazz and Fuji, unless otherwise indicated.

- *Apricots:* Select the sweetest apricot variety you can find.

- *Avocados:* Choose avocados that are neither too firm nor too ripe. Never buy one with visible spots.

- *Bananas:* Select bananas with completely yellow outer peels. Bananas are high in carbohydrates, so don't overdo it!

- *Blackberries:* Of the two blackberry varieties, only the Oregon Thornless is sweet. The Himalaya Giant is rather tart. Ask your grocer for help distinguishing between the two.

- *Blueberries:* Blueberries grow wild in mountainous regions; when they are cultivated, their flavor is blander.

- *Cherries:* There are many different types of cherries available. Choose the sweetest variety you can find.

- *Currants:* White currents (originally from Scandinavia) are much sweeter than red currants, which are rather tart.

- *Figs:* Either purple or green figs will work well in desserts.

- *Grapefruit:* We only use pink grapefruit; the white variety, although juicier, is usually more bitter.

- *Grapes:* Choose sweet and flavorful grapes for baking. A freshly picked bunch of grapes has supple branches and the stems attached to the grapes are uniform in color.

- *Kiwifruit:* Use only perfectly ripe kiwis. Unripe kiwis have no flavor and the over-ripe fruit doesn't taste very good.

- *Lemons:* Choose organic lemons that have not been treated with chemicals.

- *Limes:* While more flavorful than lemons, limes are also more tart.

- *Mangos:* Some of the best mangos come from Peru, Brazil or Côte d'Ivoire.

- *Melons:* A ripe melon is heavy, highly fragrant and separates easily from the stem. When using melons in fruit salads, serve them well chilled.

- *Oranges:* Table oranges are sweeter than oranges intended for juice.

- *Passion fruit:* You can use passion fruit with either yellow or brown skin; they taste the same.

- *Peaches:* We primarily use white peaches, which are sweeter and more aromatic than yellow peaches. Always remove the skin from chemically treated peaches, as it may contain toxins. To peel peaches, blanch them in boiling water for 30 seconds, plunge them into ice water, then peel.

- *Pears:* Comice and Conference pears are among the sweetest varieties. If you cannot find them, use the sweetest variety available.

- *Pineapples:* If possible, use Queen Victoria pineapples, which are very flavorful and naturally sweet. Avoid pineapples with abundant tall leaves, as they are usually more acidic.

- *Plums:* We prefer greengage plums for their lush sweetness when ripe and, for baking, quetsches (French prune plums).

- *Raspberries:* Because raspberries are very delicate, wash them with a light spray of water so they don't break apart, and drain them immediately. There are many varieties; the largest ones usually don't have a lot of flavor.

- *Rhubarb:* Long used in China as a medicinal plant, rhubarb is today a delicious ingredient in desserts such as sorbets, compotes, ice creams and muffins. It is often combined with apples or berries, or prepared with maple syrup.

- *Strawberries:* There are more than 20 varieties of strawberries. Wild strawberries are the sweetest and most aromatic, but are also the most delicate.

- *Tangerines and clementines:* Look for seedless, aromatic varieties.

Dried Fruit

Rehydrate all dried fruits in warm water before using them. Five to 10 minutes should be enough.

- *Apricots:* The best dried apricots come from either California or Turkey. Before using them in tarts or flans, rehydrate them in water.

- *Dates:* Choose the softest dates; otherwise, they won't have much flavor. Dates are high in carbohydrates, so eat them once or twice a week, at most.

- *Figs:* The finest dried figs come from Turkey; those from Italy and Greece are not as soft.

- *Prunes:* If you can, buy prunes with the pit still in; pitted prunes are chemically treated. Before use, soak them in water or tea for at least 15 minutes to plump them and restore their flavor.

- *Raisins:* Black Corinth raisins are the sweetest and most aromatic.

Nuts

- *Almonds:* We mainly use slivered almonds, as well as ground almonds mixed into flour to enhance the flavor of pastry, cakes and cookies. Almond milk is also a nice ingredient for baking; just be sure there is no sugar added.

- *Coconut:* We use unsweetened shredded or desiccated coconut and, in some recipes, canned coconut milk.

- *Hazelnuts:* Chopped hazelnuts provide added crunch; ground hazelnuts are used like ground almonds.

- *Pecans:* The fruit of the pecan tree, which grows primarily in eastern North America, pecans enhance many dessert recipes.

- *Pistachios:* We use whole, unsalted blanched pistachios.

- *Walnuts:* You can find walnuts year-round, but make sure they are fresh. Walnuts go rancid very quickly.

Dairy Products

- *Milk:* The cows producing milk these days have often been given antibiotics. That's why it's better to use organic milk. Because dairy products are consumed in excessive amounts in Western society, and many people have developed lactose intolerance, we prefer to use soy milk.

- *Cream:* Use half-and-half (10%) or table (18%) cream unless otherwise specified.

- *Ricotta:* Unless otherwise indicated, we use smooth, light ricotta to limit fat content.

- *Yogurt:* We use only unsweetened low-fat natural yogurt. Buy good-quality yogurt without added gelatin or stabilizers.

Oils and Fats

- *Butter:* We use light butter containing 40% to 65% fat and regular butter in some recipes where it is important for texture. We never use margarine because it's more processed.

- *Oils:* If a recipe allows, we prefer to use hazelnut oil for its wonderful flavor. Otherwise, we use sesame oil, which has a more neutral taste. Both have excellent health benefits, as they contain omega-3 and omega-6 essential fatty acids. After opening, store them in the refrigerator to keep them from going rancid.

Herbs and Spices

- *Cardamom:* An aromatic spice native to India, cardamom can be traced back to 700 BC, when it was grown in the Hanging Gardens of Babylon. It helps soothe digestion and prevents gas. Its pleasant taste deliciously flavors baked goods.

- *Cinnamon:* We use both ground cinnamon and cinnamon sticks, but never cinnamon extract, because it has added sugar.

- *Cloves:* These have a pungent taste and pair well with cinnamon, flavoring nut-based baked goods beautifully.

- *Ginger:* With its sweet and spicy flavor, ginger is delicious in cookies, cakes and other baked goods. We generally use organic ground ginger, which can be found in natural foods stores.

- *Lavender:* Because lavender is extremely fragrant, it should be used sparingly in baked goods. Lavender honey is also very aromatic.

- *Mint:* There are several varieties of mint. Use peppermint in chocolate-based desserts and bergamot (or lemon) mint in fruit salads.

- *Rose petals:* Once dried and ground into powder, rose petals can be used as a spice to give creamy desserts, ice cream and sorbets a delicate flavor.

- *Vanilla:* We only use fresh vanilla beans, as vanilla extract contains alcohol and sugar. Vanilla has a sweet aroma and flavor.

Flours and Starches

- *Whole wheat flour:* We use whole wheat flour to make pie crusts, or we combine it with all-purpose flour to make cakes, muffins, scones and cookies (because it creates a denser product, it can't be used on its own for these kinds of baked goods).

- *All-purpose flour:* This highly processed flour is lower in fiber and has more calories than whole wheat flour. Instead of using it on its own, mix all-purpose flour with whole wheat flour for baked goods that need to rise.

- *Oat flour and rolled oats:* Oats help lower cholesterol and reduce the risk of heart disease. We use both oat flour and rolled oats.

- *Cornmeal and cornstarch:* Buy superfine cornmeal to make cookies. Cornstarch is used to thicken sauces.

- *Rice flour:* We use only brown rice flour. Unlike white rice, brown rice contains vitamins B_1 and B_2, iron and magnesium. You can find brown rice flour in well-stocked health food stores.

• *Buckwheat flour:* We use buckwheat flour to make crêpes, pancakes and blinis.

• *Chestnut flour:* We mix chestnut flour with other types of flour to make crêpes and other baked goods. It's rich in potassium and vitamin C.

Chocolate and Cocoa

• *Chocolate:* You can use unsweetened chocolate, found in health food stores and in the baking section of supermarkets.. Add a natural sugar (stevia, xylitol or agave syrup) to sweeten it.

• *Unsweetened cocoa powder:* In 1828, Van Houten of the Netherlands invented cocoa powder, and the Van Houten brand of cocoa continues to be among the best on the market in Europe. Always buy high-quality Dutch-process unsweetened cocoa powder to make your desserts. Add a natural sugar (stevia, xylitol or agave syrup) to sweeten it.

Tea

We use only green tea, which gives a wonderful aroma to ice cream, creamy desserts and mousses. The finest green teas come from the Hangzhou province of China, where tea is fried in large pans in front of shops. Unlike other teas, green tea is not fermented.

Eggs

If at all possible, buy organic eggs from free-range chickens. Avoid eggs with dirty shells, as germs can penetrate through the shell to the inside of an egg. Store eggs on the shelves of the refrigerator (not the door) and, of course, make sure they are very fresh when you're using them for baking.

Pastry

• *Phyllo pastry:* Phyllo (or filo) pastry contains little fat, which makes it ideal for light desserts. It is sold in sheets and can be found in supermarkets or ethnic food markets in the freezer section. Once the package is opened, wrap tightly and store in the refrigerator for up to 3 days.

• *Brik pastry:* "Brik" (or brick) pastry is a very thin pastry from Tunisia made with semolina that is boiled, then cooked with olive oil. Look for it in supermarkets or ethnic food markets. Once the package is opened, wrap tightly and store in the refrigerator for up to 3 days.

Pies and Tarts

Pâte Brisée (Pie Dough)

Makes 9 oz (270 g) dough

This is the crust we use in most of our tart recipes. We add an egg yolk to make the dough more tender.

Tip

Follow the method at right for a melt-in-your mouth crust. If possible, let it rest in the refrigerator for 2 hours. Letting dough chill stretches it out, rendering it supple and malleable. It then rolls out more easily and doesn't shrink while baking.

⅓ cup	light butter, softened	75 mL
1	egg yolk	1
Pinch	salt	Pinch
5 tbsp	soy milk or skim milk, at room temperature	65 mL
¾ cup	whole wheat flour	175 mL

1. In a bowl, cream butter, then add egg yolk, salt and milk and stir until well blended. Slowly add flour, stirring constantly.

2. When the dough starts to come together into a ball, pat it into a flattened disk. Wrap in a clean dish towel or plastic wrap and refrigerate for at least 30 minutes or for up to 2 hours before using.

Ground Almond Pie Dough

Tip

Flour is perishable — after a month it becomes dehydrated and could ruin a recipe. Always use the freshest flour possible.

Variation

If you want to flavor the dough, add 1 tsp (5 mL) ground cinnamon with the salt.

1/3 cup	light butter, softened	75 mL
1	egg yolk	1
Pinch	salt	Pinch
5 tbsp	soy milk or skim milk, at room temperature	65 mL
1/2 cup	whole wheat flour	125 mL
1/4 cup	ground almonds	50 mL

1. In a bowl, cream butter, then add egg yolk, salt and milk and stir until well blended. Slowly add flour and ground almonds, stirring constantly.
2. Gather into a ball, wrap in plastic wrap and refrigerate for 30 minutes before using.

Pâte Sablée (Tart Dough)

For best results, every ingredient in a recipe must be of perfect quality and freshness.

Tip

Don't knead the dough for too long or it will become tough.

Variation

You can add 1/2 tsp (2 mL) of ground cinnamon to flavor this dough.

3/4 cup	whole wheat flour	175 mL
1/4 cup	light butter, softened, cut into pieces	50 mL
1	egg	1

1. Place flour on a work surface. With the tips of your fingers, rub butter into flour until butter is no longer visible and the mixture resembles coarse meal.
2. Make a well in the center and break the egg into it, then work in with your fingertips. Do not overmix. Knead dough with the palm of your hand until uniform. Gather into a ball and wrap in plastic wrap. Refrigerate for 1 hour before using.

Apple and Cranberry Cobbler

Serves 4

Cobbler is a traditional dish in both the United States and the United Kingdom, although the meaning of the word is quite different in each country. In the United States, it usually means a dessert consisting of a fruit filling and a thick biscuit crust. In the United Kingdom, it is usually a savory meat dish, typically a lamb casserole, covered with a savory scone-like topping, with each scone (or biscuit) forming a separable cobbler.

- Preheat oven to 425°F (220°C)
- 11- by 7-inch (28 by 18 cm) glass baking dish, sprayed with cooking spray

Crust

¾ cup	all-purpose flour	175 mL
1 tbsp	cornmeal	15 mL
3 tbsp	chilled butter, cut into small pieces	45 mL
2 tbsp	water	25 mL
1 tsp	lemon juice	5 mL

Filling

3 tbsp	xylitol OR	45 mL
2 tbsp	agave syrup	25 mL
1 tsp	all-purpose flour	5 mL
½ tsp	ground cinnamon	2 mL
5 cups	thinly sliced peeled sweet-tart apples	1.25 L
½ cup	dried cranberries	125 mL

1. *Prepare the crust:* In a bowl, combine flour, cornmeal, butter, water and lemon juice until smooth and soft (do not form a ball). Press gently into a 2-inch (5 cm) thick circle, wrap in plastic wrap and refrigerate for 15 minutes or until plastic can be easily removed.

2. *Prepare the filling:* In a large bowl, combine the natural sugar of your choice, flour and cinnamon. Add apples and cranberries, tossing well to coat. Spoon into prepared baking dish.

3. Place dough on a lightly floured work surface and roll into a 12- by 8-inch (30 by 20 cm) rectangle. Fit over the filling, fold edges over the edge of the dish and flute edges. Cut several slits in the top to allow steam to escape.

4. Bake in preheated oven for 30 minutes or until crust is golden brown. Let cool on a wire rack for 10 minutes before serving.

Cherry Cobbler "Maxi"

This cobbler is inspired by the rustic English apple pie. We dedicate it to Maxi, our cherished kitty, who is quite a sophisticated eater.

Tips

We make our own bread crumbs from toasted whole wheat bread.

If the cobbler is not sweet enough for your taste, you can drizzle a spoonful of maple syrup on each serving.

If stevia is available as a sweetener in your area, you can use it in this recipe by dissolving a pinch of stevia extract powder (or the equivalent of 1 tbsp/15 mL sugar) in 1 tbsp (15 mL) warm water and combining it with the cherries.

Variation

You can use chopped apples, pears or rhubarb in place of the cherries. If using rhubarb, add more natural sugar of your choice, sweetening it to taste.

- *Preheat oven to 400°F (200°C)*
- *8-inch (20 cm) soufflé dish, buttered*

¼ cup	fine bread crumbs	50 mL
2 cups	sweet cherries, pitted	500 mL
1 tbsp	liquid honey or xylitol OR	15 mL
2 tsp	agave syrup	10 mL
2 tbsp	butter, cut into pieces	25 mL
¾ cup	whole wheat flour	175 mL
2	eggs	2
1 cup + 2 tbsp	skim milk or soy milk	275 mL
¼ cup	raisins	50 mL
	Grated zest of 1 orange	

1. Sprinkle soufflé dish with bread crumbs; set aside.

2. In a bowl, combine cherries and the natural sugar of your choice. Transfer to prepared dish and dot with butter. Bake in preheated oven for 20 minutes.

3. Meanwhile, place flour in a large bowl and make a well in the center. Add eggs to the well, then slowly pour in milk, stirring constantly. Stir in raisins and orange zest. You should have a thick, pancake-like batter.

4. Reduce oven temperature to 375°F (190°C). Pour batter over cherries and bake for 40 to 45 minutes or until puffed, golden brown and crusty around the edges. Serve immediately.

Minute Pear Crumble

Crumbles are a British invention. We prepare this crumble with rolled oats, almonds and hazelnuts so that it is healthier and serve it in individual ramekins. Try it with light ricotta cheese dolloped on top.

Tip

If stevia is available as a sweetener in your area, you can use it in this recipe by combining a pinch of stevia extract powder (or the equivalent of 1 tbsp/15 mL sugar) with the oil.

Variation

You can replace the pears with apples or 1 1/2 cups (375 mL) chopped rhubarb. If using rhubarb, add the natural sugar of your choice to the filling, sweetening it to taste.

• *Two 1-cup (250 mL) ramekins*

Filling

2	ripe sweet pears, peeled and thinly sliced	2
1/2 tsp	ground cinnamon	2 mL
1 tsp	lemon juice	5 mL

Crumble

1 tbsp	vegetable oil	15 mL
1 tbsp	xylitol OR	15 mL
2 tsp	agave syrup	10 mL
1/2 cup	large-flake (old-fashioned) rolled oats	125 mL
2 tbsp	crushed hazelnuts	25 mL
1 tbsp	sliced almonds	15 mL
2 tbsp	ground almonds	25 mL

1. *Prepare the filling:* In a small saucepan, combine pears, cinnamon and lemon juice. Cook over low heat, stirring often, for 7 to 10 minutes or until pears are softened and liquid is absorbed.

2. *Meanwhile, prepare the crumble:* In another small saucepan, heat oil and the natural sugar of your choice over low heat. Add oats and sauté for 3 minutes or until golden. Add hazelnuts and sliced almonds and sauté for 2 to 3 minutes or until browned. Remove from heat and stir in ground almonds.

3. Spread filling in ramekins and sprinkle with crumble. Serve hot.

Chloe's Apple and Strawberry Crumble

Serves 4	

This version of crumble contains lots of fiber and very little fat. Moreover, strawberries and apples are an excellent source of vitamins. Serve some plain low fat yogurt on top.

Variation

You can replace the apples with pears and the strawberries with another red fruit, such as raspberries.

- *Preheat oven to 350°F (180°C)*
- *8-inch (20 cm) soufflé dish, buttered*

2	large sweet apples, peeled and cut into thin wedges	2
1¼ cups	strawberries	300 mL
	Juice of 1 orange	
½ tsp	ground cinnamon	2 mL
½ cup	large-flake (old-fashioned) rolled oats	125 mL
¼ cup	whole wheat flour	50 mL
2 tbsp	melted light butter	25 mL

1. In a bowl, combine apples, strawberries, orange juice and cinnamon. Transfer to prepared soufflé dish.
2. In another bowl, combine oats, flour and butter. Spread over fruit.
3. Bake in preheated oven for 40 to 45 minutes or until golden.

Princess Valy Chocolate Pie

At a famous New York pastry shop, steps from Central Park, we tried a raisin tart that didn't exactly suit our taste. But it does deserve credit for having inspired us to create this delicious chocolate pie — a real treat for all gourmands! We serve it warm, topped with sorbet or light whipped cream.

Tips

We rinse and drain all dried fruit before use.

If stevia is available as a sweetener in your area, you can use it in this recipe by dissolving $\frac{1}{8}$ tsp (0.5 mL) stevia extract powder (or the equivalent of 2 tbsp/ 25 mL sugar) in 1 tbsp (15 mL) extra cold water and adding it with the cocoa.

- **Preheat oven to 375°F (190°C).**
- **8-inch (20 cm) tart pan (preferably with removable bottom), buttered**

14 oz	Pâte Brisée (see recipe, page 16)	420 g
$\frac{2}{3}$ cup	pitted dates	150 mL
$\frac{2}{3}$ cup	dried figs	150 mL
$\frac{2}{3}$ cup	raisins	150 mL
	Grated zest of 1 orange	
$\frac{3}{4}$ cup	freshly squeezed orange juice	175 mL
$1\frac{3}{4}$ cups	cold water, divided	425 mL
$\frac{1}{4}$ cup	unsweetened cocoa powder	50 mL
3 tbsp	cornstarch	45 mL
$\frac{1}{2}$ tsp	spice blend of ground cardamom, cinnamon and cloves	2 mL
2 tbsp	xylitol	25 mL
	OR	
4 tsp	agave syrup	20 mL
	Grated zest of 1 lime	
1	egg, beaten	1

1. Roll out two-thirds of the dough to an 8-inch (20 cm) circle between two pieces of parchment paper and fit into prepared tart pan. Trim the excess and refrigerate for 30 minutes.

2. In a saucepan, combine dates, figs, raisins, orange juice and $\frac{1}{4}$ cup (50 mL) water. Cook over medium heat, stirring occasionally, for 2 minutes.

3. In a bowl, combine 6 tbsp (90 mL) of the cold water, cocoa powder, cornstarch, spice blend and the natural sugar of your choice. Gradually add the rest of the cold water, stirring until well blended. Pour over the date mixture. Bring to a boil, stirring constantly. Reduce heat to low and simmer, stirring, for 5 minutes. Remove from heat. Stir in orange zest and lime zest and let cool.

4. Meanwhile, preheat oven to 375°F (190°C).

5. Roll out the remaining dough to a circle 1 inch
   (2.5 cm) larger than the tart pan. Fill the pie shell
   with the cooled fruit mixture, brush the rim with
   beaten egg, then cover with the top crust. With
   lightly moistened fingers, press the top and bottom
   pieces of the crust together to seal. Make a few
   holes in the top crust. Brush with beaten egg.

6. Bake for 40 minutes or until pastry is golden. Serve
   hot or let cool

The Tournelles' Apple Pie

The La Tournelles were a family of French noblemen, and many Parisian streets are named after them — including the street we live on. The apple pie is an English variation of the French tarte Tatin. Dating back to the 14th century, apple pie did not originally contain sugar. Figs were added, as were spices such as cloves, cinnamon and even saffron and pepper! We even found a recipe from Venice made with diced bacon. We steered clear of such an "extravagance" in our recipe.

Tip

To make this delicious pie look extra-pretty, make diagonal cuts along the outside edges of the crust before baking.

- *Preheat oven to 480°F (250°C)*
- *Baking sheet, lined with parchment paper and lightly floured*

¹⁄₂ cup	Black Corinth or other dark raisins	125 mL
4	sweet apples	4
¹⁄₄ tsp	ground cinnamon	1 mL
¹⁄₄ tsp	ground cardamom	1 mL
2 tbsp	butter	25 mL
³⁄₄ cup	very fine white bread crumbs	175 mL
14 oz	Pâte Brisée (see recipe, page 16)	420 g
1¹⁄₂ cups	walnut halves, coarsely chopped	375 mL
1	egg, beaten	1
	Light whipped cream, light ricotta cheese or fromage blanc	

1. In a bowl, soak raisins in warm water for 15 minutes. Drain well and return to bowl.

2. Peel and finely grate the apples. Add to the drained raisins. Stir in cinnamon and cardamom; set aside.

3. In a skillet, melt butter over low heat. Add bread crumbs and sauté until nicely toasted.

4. On a floured work surface, roll out dough to ¹⁄₄-inch (0.5 cm) thickness and divide into two squares. Place one square on prepared baking sheet and sprinkle with bread crumbs and walnuts. Top with apple mixture, spreading evenly and leaving a 1-inch (2.5 cm) border. Roll the edges slightly inward and brush with beaten egg. Place the second square of dough on top and seal by brushing the edges with beaten egg or warm water. Using a very thin knife, score the top in a crisscross pattern.

5. Bake in preheated oven for 20 minutes. Reduce oven temperature to 400°F (200°C) and bake for about 30 minutes or until golden brown. Serve warm, topped with whipped cream.

Low-Calorie Apple Pie

Here's a lighter version of the traditional English apple pie, courtesy of our friend Anna from Nottingham. To make it even lighter, increase the amount of fruit and reduce the amount of dough. Don't add sugar, but do use good-quality sweet apple varieties that are in season and perfectly ripe.

Tips

For the spice blend, try 50% cinnamon, 40% ginger and 10% cloves, but feel free to play with it until you find a blend you like.

This pie is best served hot. It's not easy to remove from the pan, so use either a pan with a removable bottom or a silicone tart pan (no need to butter the silicone pan, of course).

- **8-inch (20 cm) tart pan with removable bottom, buttered, or silicone tart pan**

Crust

¾ cup	whole wheat flour	175 mL
¼ cup	light butter, softened	50 mL
3 tbsp	cold water	45 mL

Filling

3 tbsp	raisins	45 mL
4	large sweet apples	4
½ tsp	spice blend of ground cinnamon, ginger and cloves	2 mL
1 tbsp	liquid honey	15 mL

1. *Prepare the crust:* Place flour and butter in a bowl. Using your fingers, rub the butter into the flour until mixture resembles fine bread crumbs. Add cold water a little bit at a time, stirring after each addition. Gather dough into a ball, wrap in a clean dish towel or plastic wrap and refrigerate for 30 minutes.

2. On a lightly floured work surface, roll out dough to a circle 2½ inches (6 cm) wider than the tart pan. Cut a 1-inch (2.5 cm) wide ring around the outside of the dough. Using a brush or your fingers, moisten the rim of the pan with water and secure the ring of dough over the rim, pressing the edges firmly. Set aside.

3. *Prepare the filling:* In a bowl, soak raisins in warm water for 15 minutes. Drain well and return to bowl.

4. Peel and grate the apples. Add to the drained raisins. Stir in spice blend and honey. Pour into the bottom of the tart pan, forming a mound in the center (this is the "heart" of the pie).

5. Place the circle of dough on top of the filling and cut out a hole in the center. Moisten the edge of the dough and pinch to seal it to the ring already in place. Refrigerate for 30 minutes.

6. Meanwhile, preheat oven to 350°F (180°C).

7. Brush dough with water. Bake for 30 to 35 minutes or until top is golden brown.

Crispy Little Apple Pie Cups

Makes 4 pie cups

Here's a fun way to make small crispy pies for kids as an after-school snack. You can vary the filling depending on the season. With phyllo dough, they take only a few minutes to make.

Tip
In the summertime, serve these pie cups hot, topped with a scoop of apple or pear sorbet.

- *Preheat oven to 410°F (210°C)*
- *4 muffin cups, buttered or greased*

1	sweet apple	1
1	sweet pear	1
1 tbsp	orange juice	15 mL
¼ cup	light butter, melted (or 2 tbsp/25 mL hazelnut oil)	50 mL
4	sheets phyllo dough	4
1 tsp	ground cinnamon	5 mL

1. Peel apple and pear and coarsely grate into a bowl. Sprinkle with orange juice and set aside.

2. Cut each phyllo sheet into quarters and brush each piece with melted butter. Stack four pieces of the phyllo inside each muffin cup, staggering the points. Lightly bend the overhanging edges outward. Spoon the apple mixture into the bottom of each cup and sprinkle with cinnamon.

3. Bake for 12 to 15 minutes or until pastry is golden.

Apple, Prune and Pear Tart

Serves 6

When berries are no longer in season, we love mixing apples, prunes and pears together to make a winter dessert. The combination makes delicious compotes and tart fillings.

Tip

Naturally sweet fruits don't need any added sugar. Always select ripe, high-quality fruit.

- 8-inch (20 cm) tart pan (preferably with removable bottom), buttered

5	large prunes, pitted	5
4	sweet apples, peeled and chopped	4
1/8 tsp	ground cinnamon	0.5 mL
9 oz	Quick Puff Pastry Dough or Puff Pastry Dough (see recipe, page 46 or 47)	270 g
2 to 3	large sweet pears	2 to 3

1. Soak prunes in warm water for 30 minutes. Drain before using.

2. In a saucepan, combine apples and 1 cup (250 mL) water. Cook over medium heat, stirring, for about 20 minutes or until softened. Stir in prunes and cinnamon and cook, stirring, until water is absorbed. Let cool.

3. Preheat oven to 400°F (200°C).

4. On a lightly floured work surface, roll out dough to 1/4-inch (0.5 cm) thickness and fit into prepared tart pan. Press the edges firmly to the pan so the dough doesn't fall back down the sides. Prick the bottom with a fork.

5. Spread a layer of the apple mixture over the bottom of the crust (not too thin but not too thick — just enough to cover the bottom generously; if you have any left, you can use it as compote).

6. Peel pears, slice them very thinly and arrange them, overlapping slightly, on top of the compote, starting on the outside and working in.

7. Bake for 25 to 30 minutes or until golden. Check often during the last few minutes to make sure the edges don't burn.

Pear Tart Delight

I'm always on the lookout for the "perfect" pear tart. All of the ones I've tried have left me unsatisfied. I often dream about a heavenly pear tart, probably because the pear tree in our garden produces such delicious pears. Here is my favorite pear tart recipe to date.

Tips

The stack of phyllo gives this tart a festive look. A glass of Champagne would complement this pear delight very nicely.

Instead of the xylitol, you can use 2 tsp (10 mL) agave syrup.

If stevia is available as a sweetener in your area, you can use it in this recipe by adding a pinch of stevia extract powder (or the equivalent of 1 tbsp/15 mL sugar) and 1 tbsp (15 mL) extra water.

- *Preheat oven to 400°F (200°C)*
- *Two 8-inch (20 cm) tart pans, buttered*

5 to 6	sweet pears, peeled and diced	5 to 6
1 tsp	ground cinnamon	5 mL
1/3 cup	dried figs	75 mL
1/3 cup	dried apricots	75 mL
1 tbsp	xylitol	15 mL
2 tbsp	unsweetened cocoa powder	25 mL
9 oz	Pâte Brisée (see recipe, page 16)	270 g
3/4 cup	hazelnuts, coarsely chopped	175 mL
3	sheets phyllo dough	3
	Melted butter	
1	egg white, beaten	1

1. In a saucepan, combine pears, cinnamon and 1/3 cup (75 mL) water. Cook over low heat, stirring, until soft. Remove from heat.

2. In a food processor or by hand, finely chop figs and apricots until almost a paste; set aside.

3. In the top of a double boiler, over simmering water, dissolve xylitol in 1/4 cup (50 mL) water. Add cocoa and stir until thick. Stir in fig mixture and pear mixture; set aside.

4. On a lightly floured work surface, roll out dough to 1/4-inch (0.5 cm) thickness and fit into one of the prepared tart pans. Prick the bottom with a fork. Bake in preheated oven for 20 to 25 minutes or until golden. Let cool completely. Increase oven temperature to 480°F (250°C).

5. Sprinkle the cooled crust with hazelnuts. Pour in cocoa mixture and smooth the surface. Set aside.

6. In the other prepared tart pan, crinkle one phyllo sheet enough to fit in bottom and brush with melted butter. Place a second crinkled sheet on top and brush with butter. Crinkle the last sheet, place on top and brush with beaten egg white. Bake for 3 minutes or until crisp and golden.

7. Place the stack of phyllo on top of the tart. Serve hot or warm.

Banana Tart

I discovered bananas when I was 17 years old. I had never seen them before because, in my native country, foreign exchange was rare and the import of exotic fruit was prohibited. I thought this fruit was so good that I ate more than 2 lbs (1 kg) worth in one sitting — which wasn't exactly good for my figure!

Variations

You can replace the bananas with 1 cup (250 mL) prunes or dried figs.

Replace the crème fraîche with low-fat ricotta cheese or fromage blanc.

• **8-inch (20 cm) tart pan (preferably with removable bottom), buttered**

Crust

1 ⅓ cups	all-purpose flour	325 mL
½ cup	light butter, softened	125 mL
½ tsp	salt	2 mL
¼ cup	ground almonds	50 mL
1	egg	1

Filling

2	large bananas	2
2	egg yolks	2
1 cup	thick crème fraîche	250 mL

1. *Prepare the crust:* In a bowl, combine flour, butter, salt, almonds and egg. Form into a ball, wrap in plastic wrap and refrigerate for 30 minutes.

2. Meanwhile, preheat oven to 300°F (150°C).

3. On a lightly floured work surface, roll out dough to ¼-inch (0.5 cm) thickness and fit into prepared tart pan, pressing firmly around the edges. Prick the bottom with a fork. Bake for 20 minutes or until golden. Let cool completely. Increase oven temperature to 325°F (160°C).

4. *Prepare the filling:* In a bowl, mash bananas with a fork, or purée in a blender. Beat or blend in egg yolks and crème fraîche. Pour into cooled crust. Bake for 15 minutes or until set.

Banana and Chocolate Tart

Serves 6

This delicious little tart is perfect as a wintertime after-school snack for kids. We love serving it warm with berry sauce. It takes some time to make, but the final result is well worth the effort.

Tips

You can substitute 2 pears for the bananas. Peel and thinly slice the pears and poach in a little water over medium heat for 10 minutes. Drain well.

If stevia is available as a sweetener in your area, you can use it in this recipe by dissolving ⅛ tsp (0.5 mL) stevia extract powder (or the equivalent of 2 tbsp/ 25 mL sugar) in 2 tbsp (25 mL) warm water and adding it to the cocoa mixture.

- *Preheat oven to 340°F (170°C)*
- *8-inch (20 cm) tart pan with removable bottom, buttered*

9 oz	Pâte Brisée (see recipe, page 16)	270 g
2	bananas	2
	Juice of 1 lemon	
1⅔ cups	unsweetened cocoa powder	400 mL
½ cup	whipping (30% to 35%) cream	125 mL
2 tbsp	xylitol	25 mL
	OR	
4 tsp	agave syrup	20 mL
1	egg	1
1	egg yolk	1

1. On a lightly floured work surface, roll out dough to ¼-inch (0.5 cm) thickness and fit into prepared tart pan. Prick the bottom with a fork. Bake in preheated oven for 25 minutes or until golden.

2. Meanwhile, peel bananas and cut into slices. Sprinkle lightly with lemon juice to prevent them from turning brown.

3. Place banana slices in a microwave-safe container and microwave on Medium (50%) for about 2 minutes or until slightly softened. Set aside.

4. In a saucepan, combine cocoa and cream. Warm over low heat, without bringing to a boil. Stir in the natural sugar of your choice and remove from heat.

5. In a bowl, beat egg and egg yolk. Whisk into the cocoa mixture.

6. Arrange banana slices on the bottom of the hot crust and cover with the chocolate cream. Bake for 20 minutes or until filling is set.

Dried Apricot Tart

There are many apricot tart variations. This one is very simple, economical and fast. The dried apricots found in markets generally come from Turkey, the predominant apricot producer in the world. Dried apricots from California are, nevertheless, more aromatic and more tender.

Tip
You can replace the dried apricots with prunes, figs or dates.

• **8-inch (20 cm) tart pan with removable bottom, buttered**

1 1/4 cups	dried apricots	300 mL
2 cups	cold water	500 mL
10 oz	Pâte Sablée (see recipe, page 17)	300 g
	Unsweetened whipped cream	

1. Soak apricots in cold water overnight.

2. Preheat oven to 350°F (180°C).

3. Drain apricots and transfer to a saucepan. Cook over medium heat, stirring, for 10 minutes or until soft. Set aside.

4. On a very lightly floured surface, roll out two-thirds of the dough to 1/8-inch (3 mm) thickness and fit into prepared pie plate. Prick the bottom with a fork. Bake for 30 minutes or until light golden. Let cool slightly. Reduce oven temperature to 300°F (150°C).

5. Spread apricot compote over the crust. Roll out the remaining dough to a 1/4-inch (0.5 cm) thick square. Cut into 1/2-inch (1 cm) wide strips and arrange them over the compote in a tight lattice pattern.

6. Bake for 40 minutes or until golden brown. Keep an eye on it and lower the temperature if necessary. Serve warm or chilled, with unsweetened whipped cream.

Prune and Dried Fig Tart

Serves 6

We make this tart in the winter by soaking the prunes and figs overnight in green tea infused with lemon zest and cinnamon.

Tip

This tart is just as good made with Pâte Sablée (see recipe, page 17).

• *8-inch (20 cm) tart pan with removable bottom, buttered*

¾ cup	prunes, pitted	175 mL
¾ cup	dried figs	175 mL
1 cup	chilled green tea	250 mL
1 tsp	ground cinnamon	5 mL
	Grated zest of 1 lemon	
9 oz	Pâte Brisée (see recipe, page 16)	270 g

1. Soak prunes and figs in green tea, cinnamon and lemon zest overnight.

2. Preheat oven to 340°F (170°C).

3. Transfer fruit in its liquid to a saucepan and cook over low heat, stirring often, for 15 minutes or until soft. Purée in a blender and set aside.

4. On a floured work surface, roll out two-thirds of the dough to ¼-inch (0.5 cm) thickness and fit into prepared tart pan. Prick the bottom with a fork. Bake for 25 minutes or until golden.

5. Spread fruit purée over the crust. Roll out the remaining dough to a ¼-inch (0.5 cm) thick square. Cut into ½-inch (1 cm) wide strips and arrange them over the purée in a loose lattice pattern.

6. Bake for 20 minutes or until golden. Keep an eye on it and lower the temperature if necessary.

Tahiti Tart (page 34)

Apple Puff Pastries (page 48)

Mango and Melon Phyllo Nests (page 50)

's Chocolate-Banana Napoleon (page 54)

Mixed Fruit and Nut Tart

Serves 6

This is a traditional recipe from Tunisia that we've adapted to make a lighter version. Serve this tart with mint tea as an afternoon snack.

Tip
Since dried fruit is naturally sweet, this tart doesn't need any added sugar.

- • *Preheat oven to 400°F (200°C)*
- • *8-inch (20 cm) tart pan with removable bottom, buttered*

Crust

1	egg	1
Pinch	salt	Pinch
1 1/2 cups + 1 tbsp	sifted all-purpose flour	390 mL
1/2 cup	light butter, softened, cut into pieces	125 mL

Filling

1 1/2 cups	pitted dates, finely chopped	375 mL
1 cup	dried figs, finely chopped	250 mL
1/2 cup	raisins	125 mL
1/2 cup	slivered almonds	125 mL
3	eggs	3
1/2 cup	crème fraîche	125 mL

1. *Prepare the crust:* In a bowl, beat egg and salt. Add flour and work dough until crumbly. Incorporate butter, a few pieces at a time, and continue working until dough becomes smooth.

2. On a floured work surface, roll out dough to 1/4-inch (0.5 cm) thickness and fit into prepared tart pan.

3. *Prepare the filling:* Fill crust with dates, figs, raisins and almonds. In a bowl, beat eggs and crème fraîche; pour over the fruit and nuts.

4. Bake in preheated oven for 40 minutes or until filling is set and crust is golden. Serve warm or chilled.

Tahiti Tart

* *

Serves 6

I came up with the idea for this tart while standing in line in front of our local bakery. They make delicious traditionally baked bread, but their pastries are a bit too sugary for my taste. So I've created a tart similar to one of theirs, but with fewer calories.

Tips

Buy prunes with their pits still in, without preservatives (which pitted prunes always have).

Pick very high-quality fruit that is ripe and naturally sweet.

If they're in season, you can decorate the top with a few grapes or wild strawberries.

- *Preheat oven to 375°F (190°C)*
- *8-inch (20 cm) tart pan with removable bottom, buttered*

9 oz	Pâte Brisée (see recipe, page 16)	270 g
1 cup	prunes, pitted	250 mL
5	clementines	5
1	pink grapefruit	1
3	kiwifruit	3
1	large mango	1
1	ripe sweet pineapple	1
1 1/2 cups	raspberries	375 mL
	Fresh mint leaves	

1. On a lightly floured work surface, roll out dough to 1/4-inch (0.5 cm) thickness and fit into prepared tart pan. Prick the bottom with a fork. Bake for about 20 minutes or until golden. Let cool slightly.

2. Meanwhile, in a saucepan, combine prunes and 1/3 cup (75 mL) water. Cook over low heat, stirring often, for 20 minutes or until soft. Drain and return to the pan; mash with a fork and set aside.

3. Peel clementines and grapefruit and break into segments. Scoop out little balls from the kiwis and mangos using a melon baller and cut pineapple into thin slices; set aside.

4. Unmold crust onto a platter. Spread the prune compote over the crust and generously top with fruit. To decorate, top with raspberries and a few mint leaves.

Midsummer's Dream Tart

We created this tart for our Canadian friends. It's very quick to make and is delicious, served cold, on a summer afternoon while you're sipping tea in the garden.

Tip

To make this tart in winter, we use frozen blueberries and raspberries.

- **Preheat oven to 350°F (180°C)**
- **8-inch (20 cm) tart pan with removable bottom, buttered**

9 oz	Pâte Brisée (see recipe, page 16)	270 g
2 tbsp	cornstarch	25 mL
2 tbsp	cold water	25 mL
¾ cup	pure maple syrup	175 mL
	OR	
⅔ cup	agave syrup	150 mL
1 cup	crème fraîche	250 mL
¾ cup	wild strawberries	175 mL
¾ cup	blueberries	175 mL
¾ cup	raspberries	175 mL

1. On a lightly floured work surface, roll out dough to ¼-inch (0.5 cm) thickness and fit into prepared tart pan. Prick the bottom with a fork. Bake for 20 minutes or until golden. Let cool completely.

2. In a saucepan, combine cornstarch and cold water. Stir in maple syrup or agave syrup. Bring to a boil over medium heat, stirring constantly, and boil for 5 minutes. Let cool.

3. Unmold crust onto a platter. Spread the syrup mixture over the bottom of the crust.

4. Whip crème fraîche until firm. Spread over syrup layer. Top with strawberries, blueberries and raspberries. Refrigerate for 1 hour.

Tart with Pine Nuts and Honey

Serves 4

The word "tart" occurs in a 14th-century book of recipes, relating to a savory recipe with meat. In modern North America, a tart is usually a dessert pie.

Tip
This dessert is better when served hot.

- *Preheat oven to 350°F (180°C)*
- *Baking sheet*
- *8-inch (20 cm) tart pan with removable bottom, buttered*

9 oz	Pâte Brisée (see recipe, page 16)	270 g
²⁄₃ cup	liquid honey	150 mL
	OR	
½ cup	agave syrup	125 mL
6 tbsp	butter, softened	90 mL
3	eggs, lightly beaten	3
¼ tsp	vanilla extract	1 mL
1 tbsp	amaretto (Italian bitter almond liqueur)	15 mL
1 tsp	finely grated lemon zest	5 mL
1 tsp	lemon juice	5 mL
1 cup	pine nuts, toasted	250 mL

1. Slide baking sheet into the center of the oven.

2. Roll out dough between two sheets of waxed paper to ¼-inch (0.5 cm) thickness and fit into prepared tart pan. Prick the bottom with a fork. Refrigerate for 15 minutes. Bake on the baking sheet in preheated oven for about 10 minutes or until pastry turns white.

3. Meanwhile, in a saucepan, heat honey (if using) over low heat until liquefied. Remove from heat.

4. In a bowl, beat butter until smooth. Beat in eggs in three additions, continuing to beat after each addition. Beat in honey or agave syrup, vanilla, amaretto, lemon zest and lemon juice. Stir in pine nuts. Pour into crust and smooth the surface.

5. Place the pan on the hot baking sheet and bake for 25 minutes. Cover with foil and bake for 15 minutes or until filling is set.

Maple Syrup Tart

Maple syrup is especially delicious with crêpes, waffles and pancakes. We use just a little, due to its high carbohydrate content. But we couldn't get away from the delicious maple syrup tart, though we tried to reduce the calories as much as possible.

Variations

You can also use low-fat ricotta cheese or fromage blanc in place of the compote.

Substitute ³⁄₄ cup (175 mL) agave syrup for the maple syrup.

- *Preheat oven to 350°F (180°C)*
- *8-inch (20 cm) tart pan with removable bottom, buttered*

9 oz	Pâte Brisée (see recipe, page 16)	270 g
2 tbsp	cornstarch	25 mL
2 tbsp	cold water	25 mL
1 cup	pure maple syrup	250 mL
1 cup	Apple Compote with Red Fruits (see recipe, page 147)	250 mL

1. On a lightly floured work surface, roll out dough to ¹⁄₄-inch (0.5 cm) thickness and fit into prepared tart pan. Prick the bottom with a fork. Bake for 20 minutes or until golden. Let cool completely.

2. In a saucepan, combine cornstarch and cold water. Stir in maple syrup. Bring to a boil over low heat, stirring constantly, and boil for 5 minutes. Let cool.

3. Spread maple syrup mixture over the bottom of the crust. Top with apple compote.

Vivi's Custard Tart

• •

Serves 6

Prunes were highly prized by sailors in the 17th and 18th centuries because they retained their fruit properties and prevented scurvy during long excursions. According to legend, the "prune d'Ente" (a French plum cultivar), a unique variety that becomes Agen prunes once dried, was brought from Damascus to southwestern France by Eleanor of Aquitaine upon her return from the Second Crusade in 1149.

Variations

When plums are in season, use them in place of the prunes.

This is just as delicious with banana slices in place of the pears. Do not cook them — just arrange them as with the pear quarters.

• *Preheat oven to 410°F (210°C)*
• *8-inch (20 cm) tart pan with removable bottom, buttered*

9 oz	Pâte Brisée (see recipe, page 16)	270 g
Filling		
4	large ripe sweet pears	4
1½ cups	prunes, pitted	375 mL
Custard		
⅓ cup	cornstarch	75 mL
2	eggs	2
2 cups	soy milk or skim milk	500 mL
¼ cup	raisins	50 mL
1½ tbsp	light butter	22 mL
1 tsp	vanilla extract	5 mL

1. On a lightly floured work surface, roll out dough to ¼-inch (0.5 cm) thickness and fit into prepared tart pan. Prick the bottom with a fork. Bake in preheated oven for 15 minutes or until light golden. Let cool completely.

2. *Prepare the filling:* Peel pears and cut lengthwise into quarters. In a saucepan, combine pears, prunes and 3 cups (750 mL) water. Cook over medium heat, stirring often, for 20 minutes or until soft. Drain and set aside.

3. *Prepare the custard:* In a saucepan, whisk together cornstarch, eggs and milk. Bring to a boil over low heat, stirring constantly. Add raisins and boil gently for 2 to 3 minutes. Remove from heat, stir in butter and vanilla and let cool to lukewarm.

4. Meanwhile, preheat broiler.

5. Pour half the custard into the bottom of the crust. Arrange pear quarters around the outer edge and prunes in the middle. Pour the remaining custard on top. Place tart under the broiler to lightly brown the surface.

Hungarian Ricotta Tart

My grandmother, who had a Hungarian family background, used to make this tart for us on special occasions.

Tips

We use aluminum cake pans as they give the best baking results.

Drain the ricotta well — it needs to be dry.

You can also use 4 tsp (20 mL) agave syrup instead of the xylitol or honey.

If stevia is available as a sweetener in your area, you can use it in this recipe by dissolving $\frac{1}{8}$ tsp (0.5 mL) stevia extract powder (or the equivalent of 2 tbsp/ 25 mL sugar) in 2 tbsp (25 mL) warm water and adding it to the ricotta mixture.

Variation

You can flavor the dough by using unsweetened apple juice or freshly squeezed orange juice in place of the water.

- **Preheat oven to 375°F (190°C)**
- **9-inch (23 cm) round aluminum cake pan, buttered**

$\frac{3}{4}$ cup	raisins	175 mL
$1\frac{1}{3}$ cups	all-purpose flour	325 mL
1 cup + 2 tbsp	whole wheat flour	275 mL
1 tsp	baking powder	5 mL
Pinch	salt	Pinch
	Grated zest of $\frac{1}{2}$ lemon	
$\frac{3}{4}$ cup	light butter, cut into small pieces	175 mL
2	egg yolks, beaten	2
$\frac{1}{2}$ cup	water	125 mL
1 lb	light ricotta cheese or fromage blanc, drained (see tip, at left)	500 g
4	eggs	4
2 tbsp	xylitol or liquid honey	25 mL

1. Soak raisins in warm water for 15 minutes, until soft. Drain and set aside.

2. Meanwhile, on a work surface, combine all-purpose and whole wheat flours and make a well in the center. Add baking powder, salt, lemon zest, butter and egg yolks to the well. Gently work with your fingertips until all the flour is incorporated. Gradually add water, working until dough is elastic.

3. On a floured work surface, roll out half the dough to a $\frac{1}{8}$-inch (3 mm) thick circle and fit into prepared pan. Roll out the remaining dough the same way and set aside.

4. In a bowl, combine ricotta, 3 of the eggs, raisins and the natural sugar of your choice. Pour over crust until it reaches $\frac{3}{4}$ inch (2 cm) from the top of the pan. Moisten the edges of the crust and cover with the other circle of dough, pressing with your fingers to seal. (If you have any dough left over, you can decorate the top with strips made from it.) Beat the remaining egg and brush over the top crust.

5. Bake in preheated oven for 40 minutes or until brown and firm.

Tuscan Rice Tarts

Serves 6

In the hills surrounding Florence, on the way to Fiesole, is an inn that is authentically Tuscan in both its decor and its cooking traditions. It was there that we discovered these delicious tarts. We left with the recipe, which the adorable innkeeper scribbled for us on a paper towel in his elegant style — needless to say, it took us quite some time to decipher it!

Tips

Enjoy these tarts warm or cold, with a glass of Vino Santo or a good Chianti.

If stevia is available as a sweetener in your area, you can use it in this recipe by combining a pinch of stevia extract powder (or the equivalent of 1 tbsp/15 mL sugar) with the cocoa.

• 6-cup muffin pan or six 2-inch (5 cm) tartlet molds

1/2 cup	short-grain rice (such as Arborio), rinsed	125 mL
1 tsp	ground cinnamon	5 mL
1 1/4 cups	milk	300 mL
	Grated zest of 1 lemon	
7 oz	Pâte Brisée (see recipe, page 16)	210 g
6	pitted dates, finely chopped	6
1 tbsp	unsalted pistachios, ground	15 mL
1	whole egg, beaten	1
1	egg yolk, beaten	1
1 tbsp	unsweetened cocoa powder	15 mL
1 tbsp	xylitol	15 mL
	OR	
2 tsp	agave syrup	10 mL

1. In a saucepan, combine rice, cinnamon and milk. Cook over low heat for 20 minutes, adding a little water or milk if needed, until rice is plump. Pour into a large bowl and let cool.

2. On a floured work surface, roll out pastry to 1/4-inch (0.5 cm) thickness. Cut out circles and line muffin cups or tartlet molds. Freeze for 15 minutes.

3. Meanwhile, preheat oven to 350°F (180°C).

4. Bake tart shells for 10 minutes or until golden.

5. Stir lemon zest, dates and pistachios into rice mixture. Fold in egg and egg yolk. Pour into tart shells. Bake for 25 minutes or until firm and golden. Let cool before removing from molds.

6. Combine cocoa and the natural sugar of your choice and sprinkle on top of the tarts.

Berry Tartlets

• •

These little tartlets can be prepared very quickly and contain plenty of vitamins.

Tips

If your berries are very sweet, you can omit the natural sugar.

Serve these tartlets freshly made with sorbet, which will slowly melt into the sauce.

If stevia is available as a sweetener in your area, you can use it in this recipe by dissolving 1/8 tsp (0.5 mL) stevia extract powder (or the equivalent of 2 tbsp/ 25 mL sugar) in 2 tbsp (25 mL) extra water and adding it to the berry mixture.

- *Preheat oven to 375°F (190°C)*
- *2-inch (5 cm) round cookie cutter*
- *Eight 2-inch (5 cm) tartlet molds, buttered*

3	sheets phyllo dough	3
1/3 cup	light butter, melted	75 mL
4 cups	berries, such as raspberries, currants, blackberries, strawberries or blueberries (about 1 lb/500 g)	1 L
2 tbsp	water	25 mL
2 tbsp	xylitol or liquid honey OR	25 mL
4 tsp	agave syrup	20 mL

1. Brush each sheet of phyllo dough with butter and stack on top of each other. Cut out 8 rounds with the cookie cutter and fit into prepared tartlet molds. Bake in preheated oven for 10 to 15 minutes or until golden brown. Set aside.

2. In a saucepan, combine berries, water and the natural sugar of your choice. Simmer over medium heat for 5 minutes or until softened. Strain berries, reserving the liquid to use as the sauce. Let cool.

3. Unmold tartlet shells and fill with fruit. Serve with sauce drizzled over each tartlet.

Happy Children Tartlets

Serves 6

We created these tartlets to replace the factory-made cakes children usually eat for an after-school snack. They are very easy to make, delectable-looking and perfectly healthy, containing few carbohydrates and no "bad" fat.

Variation

You can substitute pears for the apples.

- *Preheat oven to 400°F (200°C)*
- *3-inch (7.5 cm) round cookie cutter*
- *Six 4-inch (10 cm) tartlet molds, buttered*

6	sweet apples	6
	Juice of 1 lemon	
9 oz	Ground Almond Pie Dough (see recipe, page 17)	270 g
½ tsp	ground cinnamon	2 mL

1. Peel and chop 4 of the apples. In a saucepan, combine apples and 1 cup (250 mL) water. Cook over medium heat for 20 minutes or until soft.

2. Peel the remaining apples and thinly slice. Toss with lemon juice so they don't turn brown and set aside.

3. On a floured work surface, roll out dough to no more than ¼ inch (0.5 cm) thick. Cut out 6 rounds with the cookie cutter and fit into prepared tartlet molds.

4. Fill the bottom of the tartlet shells with a thin layer of compote, smoothing the surface. Arrange apple slices on top. Sprinkle with cinnamon. Bake in preheated oven for 15 minutes or until golden.

Fig Tartlets

Serves 6

Figs are naturally very sweet, so added sugar isn't needed. White figs have thinner skin, while purple figs have more flavor. Figs are often used in Italian pastry; in fact, we came up with the idea for these tartlets when we tried a fig tart at the famous Antico Caffè Greco, in Rome.

Tip
For the best flavor, choose high-quality figs that are very ripe. You can use either purple or white figs.

- *Preheat oven to 425°F (220°C)*
- *3-inch (7.5 cm) round cookie cutter*
- *Six 4-inch (10 cm) tartlet molds, buttered*

½ cup	slivered almonds	125 mL
1 cup	dried figs, chopped	250 mL
	Juice of ½ lime	
1 lb	ripe figs	500 g
Pinch	ground cinnamon	Pinch
9 oz	Puff Pastry Dough (see recipe, page 47)	270 g

1. In a dry skillet, toast almonds over low heat until golden brown. Set aside.

2. In a saucepan, combine dried figs and lime juice. Cook over low heat, stirring often, for 10 minutes or until soft. Remove from heat.

3. Mash fresh figs with a fork, or purée in a blender. Stir in cinnamon and the dried fig mixture. Set aside.

4. On a floured work surface, roll out dough to ¼-inch (0.5 cm) thickness. Cut out 6 rounds with the cookie cutter and fit into prepared tartlet molds.

5. Fill tartlet shells with the fig mixture. Sprinkle with toasted almonds. Bake for 15 minutes or until golden. Serve warm.

Flourless Tartlets with Ricotta and Raspberries

These tartlets are quick to make. We came up with the idea while at a market in Provence, chatting with a merchant who was selling Camembert cheese made with nuts, an intriguing find we couldn't wait to try. Here, we've created a more diet-conscious version.

Tip

We use bite-size tartlet molds to make tiny tarts to serve with tea or coffee.

Variation

You can replace the raspberries with another seasonal fruit, such as strawberries, red grapes or blackberries. In winter, mix the ricotta with pear or prune compote.

• *Eight 2½-inch (6 cm) tartlet molds, lined with parchment paper*

Base

¼ cup	hazelnuts	50 mL
8	dried apricots	8
8	dried figs	8
1 tbsp	hazelnut oil	15 mL

Filling

1 cup	raspberries	250 mL
¾ cup	light ricotta cheese or fromage blanc	175 mL

1. *Prepare the base:* In a blender, combine hazelnuts, apricots, figs and hazelnut oil. Blend to a sticky paste. Spoon into prepared tartlet molds, packing tightly to make a compact base. Refrigerate for 1 hour.

2. *Prepare the filling:* Reserve 2 tbsp (25 mL) raspberries for decoration. In a blender, purée the remaining raspberries. Transfer to a bowl and stir in ricotta.

3. Fill tartlet molds with the ricotta mixture. Decorate with the reserved raspberries and refrigerate for 3 to 4 hours or until firm.

4. When ready to serve, unmold tartlets and place on a serving dish.

Pastries

Quick Puff Pastry Dough

1 cup	all-purpose flour	250 mL
4 oz	Petit Suisses (fresh unsalted cheese) or cream cheese, cut into small pieces	125 g
¼ cup	butter, cut into small pieces	50 mL

Makes 10 oz (300 g)

Here's a recipe for a quick version of puff pastry. Even though it's super-fast and easy, It's just as delicious as traditional puff pastry.

1. Sift the flour onto a work surface and make a well in the center. Place the Petits Suisses and the butter in the well. Work the mixture with your fingertips until the dough becomes smooth.

2. Gather into a ball and roll in flour. Let rest for 20 minutes. If dough is soft, chill before rolling and baking.

Puff Pastry Dough

Makes 2 lbs (1 kg)

Real puff pastry requires a lot of time. We recommend that you prepare a larger batch than you need and freeze it. The recipe below makes 2 lbs (1 kg) of dough, enough for about four 8-inch (20 cm) tart shells.

Tip

Be sure to just lightly flour the work surface each time to prevent adding too much flour to the dough.

1 cup	cold water	250 mL
1½ tsp	salt	7 mL
2 cups	light butter, softened, divided	500 mL
1⅔ cups	all-purpose flour, sifted	400 mL
1 cup	whole wheat flour	250 mL

1. Dissolve the salt in the cold water. In a small saucepan, melt ⅓ cup (75 mL) of the butter over low heat.

2. In a bowl, combine all-purpose and whole wheat flours. Stir in melted butter, then add the salt water and mix to a smooth dough. Roll into a ball and flatten into a disk. Wrap in plastic wrap and refrigerate for 2 hours.

3. On a lightly floured work surface, roll out dough to a square about ¾-inch (2 cm) thick, leaving it thicker in the middle than around the edges.

4. In the saucepan, melt the remaining butter over low heat. Pour the butter in the center of the dough and fold each corner in toward the middle to form a square.

5. Keeping the surface lightly floured, roll out the square to make a rectangle three times longer than its width. Fold the dough in thirds as you would to make a rectangular envelope. Wrap and refrigerate for 2 hours.

6. On a lightly floured work surface, roll dough out to a rectangle and fold in thirds as before. Wrap and refrigerate for 1 hour. Repeat four more times, letting the dough rest in the refrigerator for 1 to 2 hours between each turn.

Apple Puff Pastries

• •

	Serves 8	

Inspired by and loosely adapted from a tart we had at Lenôtre in Paris, this dessert is very refined. We serve it warm, topped with sorbet, at the end of a meal. You can find recipes for ice cream and sorbets in the Frozen Desserts chapter.

Tip
The baking time in step 4 may vary depending on the oven, so be attentive and, if necessary, lower the heat to 450°F (230°C) for the final 10 minutes.

Variation
In place of the apples, you can substitute pears.

• **Baking sheet, lined with parchment paper or buttered**

8	large sweet apples	8
½ tsp	ground cinnamon	2 mL
1 cup	raisins	250 mL
	Boiling water	
14 oz	Puff Pastry Dough (see recipe, page 47)	420 g
1	egg, beaten	1
2 tbsp	butter, softened	25 mL

1. Peel and chop 4 of the apples. In a saucepan, combine apples and 1 cup (250 mL) water. Cook over medium heat for 15 minutes or until apples are soft and all of the water is absorbed. Stir in cinnamon and set aside.

2. Meanwhile, in a bowl, cover raisins in boiling water; drain and set aside.

3. Preheat oven to 480°F (250°C).

4. On a lightly floured work surface, roll puff pastry dough into a ⅛-inch (3 mm) thick rectangle. Cut into 8 equal rectangles. Place on prepared baking sheet, at least 1 inch (2.5 cm) apart. With a knife, decoratively score the surface and brush with beaten egg. Bake for 20 minutes or until golden. Set aside. Reduce oven temperature to 350°F (180°C).

5. Meanwhile, peel the remaining apples and cut in half lengthwise. Thinly slice, keeping the shape of the apples intact. Brush the sliced apples with butter and place on a baking sheet. Bake for about 15 minutes or until tender (they should not break apart or turn too brown). Let cool.

6. When ready to serve, preheat the broiler.

7. Split the puff pastry rectangles in half. Spread the bottom half with the apple compote. Sprinkle with raisins. Place several apple slices on top. Cover with the puff pastry tops. Decorate the top of each pastry with the remaining apple slices and broil for 2 minutes.

Ricotta and Apple Turnovers

It was while we were in New York, eating breakfast at the famous Carnegie Deli on 7th Avenue, that we came up with the idea for this dessert. It is very easy to make, and its crunchy texture, combined with stewed apple compote and ricotta cheese, is delicious served hot or at room temperature. Excellent for a winter snack or even breakfast.

Variations

You can substitute ripe, naturally sweet pears for the apples.

Substitute Broccio, an unripened cheese from Corsica, for the ricotta.

• *Baking sheet, buttered or lined with parchment paper*

4	sweet apples	4
Pinch	ground cinnamon	Pinch
1/3 cup	raisins	75 mL
	Hot water	
1/2 cup	ricotta cheese, drained (see tip, at left)	125 mL
6	sheets phyllo dough	6
2 tbsp	light butter, melted	25 mL
1	egg, beaten	1
1/2 cup	slivered almonds, toasted	125 mL

1. Peel and chop apples. In a saucepan, combine apples and 1 cup (250 mL) water. Cook over medium heat for 15 minutes or until apples are soft and all of the water is absorbed. Stir in cinnamon and let cool.

2. Meanwhile, in a bowl, soak raisins in hot water for 10 to 15 minutes or until soft. Drain well. Stir raisins and ricotta into cooled compote.

3. Preheat oven to 350°F (180°C).

4. Unroll the phyllo sheets and cut into 6 squares. Separate the squares and brush each one with melted butter. Place three squares on top of each other. Spoon a scant 1/4 cup (50 mL) of the ricotta mixture in the middle of each square. Fold each square into a triangle, folding edges and making sure all seams are well buttered. Place on prepared baking sheet and brush tops with beaten egg. Bake for 10 to 15 minutes or until golden brown.

5. When ready to serve, sprinkle with toasted almonds.

Mango and Melon Phyllo Nests

Serves 4

The name "phyllo" comes from the Greek word phyllon, *meaning "leaf." These phyllo nests boast a lot of vitamins and antioxidants.*

Tips

You can decorate these nests with any other seasonal fruit, such as grapes, sliced strawberries or diced peaches or plums.

We serve these mini cups when they are freshly made.

- *Preheat oven to 350°F (180°C)*
- *4 muffin cups, greased*

3	sheets phyllo dough	3
¼ cup	melted butter or hazelnut oil	50 mL
1	small melon	1
1	mango	1
½ cup	sugar-free organic blueberry jam	125 mL
1 tsp	grated lemon zest	5 mL

1. Cut each phyllo sheet into four pieces and brush each with melted butter.

2. Stack phyllo sheets inside prepared muffin cups, alternating the points to make a pretty shape. Lightly bend the overhanging edges outward. Bake in preheated oven for 15 minutes or until golden. Let cool.

3. Meanwhile, scoop out small balls of melon with a melon baller or ice cream scoop. Cut large slices down the sides of the mango, then score a crisscross pattern into the flesh with a knife and cut the small cubes from the skin. Chill the fruit.

4. Place a spoonful of blueberry jam in each cup and fill with fruit. Sprinkle with lemon zest.

Little Tatins with Exotic Fruits and Apples

• •

This dessert originated in Sologne, a French region known for hunting. Sisters Stéphanie and Caroline Tatin ran a restaurant there (which still exists as the hotel restaurant Tatin), patronized by numerous hunters. One Sunday at the start of the hunt, as she was preparing one of the apple tarts for a hunter's meal, one of the sisters absentmindedly let it burn. She decided to add more pastry and put the tart back in the oven. The hunters really liked this tart, which has become known as tart Tatin.

Tips

You can vary the fruit to experiment with different flavors.

Tart Tatin is traditionally served in France with a scoop of vanilla ice cream or a little crème fraîche.

• Preheat the oven to 400°F (200°C)
• 6 small individual pie plates

¾ cup	butter, divided	175 mL
¼ cup	xylitol or liquid honey OR	50 mL
3 tbsp	agave syrup	45 mL
6	apples, peeled and chopped	6
1	mango	1
Pinch	ground cinnamon	Pinch
6	sheets phyllo dough	6
6 tbsp	ground almonds	90 mL

1. In a saucepan, melt ¼ cup (50 mL) of the butter over low heat. Add the natural sugar of your choice and let it caramelize, being careful not to overcook. Add apples and cook until lightly brown.

2. Cut the mango into large pieces and add to the pan along with 2 tbsp (25 mL) water. Sprinkle with cinnamon. Cook, stirring, for 2 minutes. Remove from heat.

3. In another saucepan, melt remaining butter over low heat and butter the molds.

4. Brush each phyllo sheet with melted butter, cut the sheets in two pieces and line the prepared molds, crisscrossing rectangles and letting the edges hang over the pie plate. Fill with fruit compote and sprinkle with almonds. Fold the edges of the phyllo over the filling and brush with butter to make the folded edges stick together. Bake in preheated oven for about 10 minutes or until phyllo is golden.

Fig Croustades

Serves 4

Fig croustades are an Asian pastry, usually made with lots of honey and butter. We've adapted the recipe to make a light, low-calorie dessert.

Tip

We serve these croustades warm, topped with a scoop of green apple or lemon sorbet. In winter, serve them with unsweetened whipped cream.

• Baking sheet, lined with parchment paper

1 ½ cups	dried figs	375 mL
½ tsp	ground cinnamon	2 mL
	Grated zest of 1 orange	
6	sheets phyllo dough	6
6 tbsp	light butter, softened	90 mL

1. In a saucepan, combine 1 cup (250 mL) water, figs, cinnamon and orange zest. Simmer over low heat, stirring often, for 40 minutes.

2. Preheat oven to 350°F (180°C).

3. Brush phyllo sheets with butter and divide them into two stacks of three sheets each. Place one stack on prepared baking sheet and spread with fig mixture. Place the remaining stack on top. Lightly crinkle the top. Brush the top with more butter. Bake for 15 minutes or until golden. Cut into squares and serve hot or at room temperature.

Vicky's Ricotta Napoleon

Serves 6

This napoleon is very easy, can be made very quickly and is certainly economical. You can also make a savory version by replacing the raisins with toasted pine nuts and lightly salting the ricotta cream.

Tips

Each layer of the ricotta mixture should be at least ¾ inch (2 cm) thick.

This delicious dessert is best served hot or warm.

- **Preheat oven to 350°F (180°C)**
- **13- by 9-inch (33 by 23 cm) baking dish, buttered**

¾ cup	raisins	175 mL
9	sheets phyllo dough	9
½ cup	light butter, melted	125 mL
4	eggs	4
1 lb	low-fat ricotta or cottage cheese, drained	500 g
	Grated zest of 1 lemon	

1. In a bowl, soak raisins in warm water for 10 minutes. Drain well.

2. Spread out the phyllo sheets on a lightly floured work surface. Separate the sheets and brush each one with melted butter. Place the sheets on top of each other in three separate stacks and lightly scrunch them, making creases.

3. In a bowl, beat 3 of the eggs and stir in ricotta, raisins and the lemon zest.

4. Place the first stack of phyllo in prepared baking dish. Pour in half the ricotta mixture. Place the second stack of phyllo over top. Pour in the remaining ricotta mixture. Finish by adding the last stack of phyllo. Moisten the edges and crimp the dough with your fingers to enclose the filling. Beat remaining egg and brush on top of the pastry. Bake in preheated oven for 15 minutes or until the top is beautifully golden.

Vlad's Chocolate-Banana Napoleon

This delicious fruit dessert should be prepared just before serving. The blend of still-warm, crunchy pastry with the melting ice cream makes it worthy of a grand restaurant.

Tip

For a lighter version, substitute pear compote for the bananas.

In place of brik pastry, use puff pastry, baking four pastry squares separately.

- *Preheat oven to 400°F (200°C)*
- *Baking sheet, lined with parchment paper*

6 tbsp	light butter	90 mL
⅓ cup	unsweetened cocoa powder	75 mL
1 tbsp	liquid honey or xylitol	15 mL
3	sheets brik pastry	3
2	bananas	2
	Juice of 1 lemon	
1½ cups	Vanilla Ice Cream with Pecans (page 184)	375 mL

1. In a saucepan, melt butter over low heat. Add cocoa and the natural sugar of your choice. Mix well to blend. Remove from heat.

2. Cut each pastry sheet into four pieces, then spread the chocolate mixture on top of each. Place on prepared baking sheet. Bake in preheated oven for 8 minutes or until golden. Let cool on pan on a rack.

3. When ready to serve, peel bananas and sprinkle with lemon juice so they don't turn brown. Mash them with a fork.

4. Spread the banana purée on one pastry sheet, place another sheet on top and spread with a layer of ice cream. Finish by placing another sheet on top. Repeat to make 4 napoleons.

Hazelnut and Chocolate Strudel

Serves 6		

The word "strudel" comes from an Austrian word that means "whirlpool," no doubt because of its shape. Apple strudel is the best known, but there are other variations, such as cherry, mango and so on. This one is our favorite.

Tip
Serve warm, topped with light whipped cream or ricotta.

- *Preheat oven to 375°F (190°C)*
- *Baking sheet, buttered or lined with parchment paper*

1 cup	pitted dates	250 mL
3/4 cup	unsweetened cocoa powder	175 mL
6 tbsp	soy milk or skim milk (approx.)	90 mL
3 tbsp	pure maple syrup	45 mL
	OR	
2 tbsp	agave syrup	25 mL
10	sheets phyllo dough	10
2/3 cup	melted butter	150 mL
1 1/4 cups	finely chopped hazelnuts	300 mL
1	egg, beaten	1

1. In a blender or food processor, finely chop dates.

2. In a small saucepan, dissolve cocoa in milk. Stir in dates and the natural sugar of your choice. Add a little more milk if necessary; the sauce should be fairly thick.

3. On a lightly floured work surface, lay out phyllo sheets and brush them with butter. Stack two sheets on top of each other, sprinkle with 1/4 cup (50 mL) of the hazelnuts and brush with chocolate sauce. Stack two more sheets on top, sprinkle with 1/4 cup (50 mL) hazelnuts and brush with chocolate. Repeat layers until you have used up all the phyllo sheets.

4. Roll up the strudel as tightly as possible and trim the ends. Place on prepared baking sheet. Brush with beaten egg and sprinkle with the remaining hazelnuts. Bake for 20 to 25 minutes or until golden. If the hazelnuts start to get too brown, cover with a sheet of parchment paper.

My Mother's Tyrolean Strudel

• •

Strudel originated in Austria but is now popular throughout the Balkan region. The dough should be elastic and very thin, almost transparent. Thin dough is so important that, in Central Europe, women often get together to show each other how they've "succeeded" in making a strudel with dough thinner than the other's. My mother was a master at it, and yes, she was very proud. Her reputation as an "expert pastry maker" spread to all the neighboring villages! Here is her recipe.

• • ◆ •• •

• **Baking sheet, lined with parchment paper and dusted with flour**

Dough

2 tsp	active dry yeast	10 mL
½ cup	milk, warmed	125 mL
2½ cups + 1 tbsp	all-purpose flour	640 mL
2	eggs	2
Pinch	salt	Pinch

Filling

¼ cup	raisins	50 mL
	Hot water	
1 lb	sweet apples	500 g
	Juice of 1 lemon	
1 tbsp	ground cinnamon	15 mL
¼ cup	butter, divided	50 mL
3 tbsp	bread crumbs	45 mL
1	egg, beaten	1

1. *Prepare the dough:* In a bowl, dissolve yeast in warm milk. Let stand for about 10 minutes or until foamy.

2. In a large bowl, form a well in the center of the flour. Beat the eggs and salt, pour into the well and mix with your fingers. Add the yeast mixture and mix until a soft dough forms. On a floured work surface, knead well and form a smooth and elastic ball that doesn't stick to the work surface or your fingers. Let the dough rest, covered, in a warm place for 1 hour.

3. On a large, lightly floured work surface, roll out dough until it is very thin. Stretch the dough out with your hands, without tearing it, until it is almost transparent. Trim the edges to make a square. Let rest.

Tips

To prevent the dough from tearing when you're handling it, roll it out onto a lightly floured cloth and then use the cloth to help roll up the log.

In Vienna, this strudel is served warm with whipped cream in the afternoon with tea or coffee.

4. Preheat oven to 400°F (200°C).

5. *Prepare the filling:* In a bowl, cover raisins with hot water and drain well. Peel and grate apples. Sprinkle with lemon juice and cinnamon and set aside.

6. In a skillet, melt 1 tbsp (15 mL) of the butter over medium heat. Sauté bread crumbs until starting to brown. Remove from heat.

7. Squeeze apples dry. Dot the dough with the remaining butter and sprinkle with bread crumbs, raisins and apples. Roll into a tight log and seal the ends by lightly moistening the edges and pressing firmly with your fingers. Brush the log with beaten egg. Transfer to prepared baking sheet. Bake for 25 minutes or until golden. Let cool before slicing.

Quick Low-Calorie Spice Strudel

Serves 6

Here's another strudel made with phyllo, so it can be whipped up in a matter of minutes. We've replaced the bread crumbs with finely chopped walnuts. Strudels are best when served warm.

Variations

Prepare a savory version of this strudel, filled with ricotta or fromage blanc, for example, or with spinach, ricotta and pine nuts.

When cherries are in season, replace the apples with 2 cups (500 mL) chopped pitted cherries. Omit the lemon juice.

• *Baking sheet, buttered*

⅓ cup	raisins	75 mL
½ cup	warm water	125 mL
2	sweet apples	2
	Grated zest and juice of 1 lemon	
1 tsp	ground cinnamon	5 mL
½ tsp	ground cardamom	2 mL
½ tsp	ground ginger	2 mL
9	sheets phyllo dough	9
¼ cup	melted light butter	50 mL
½ cup	finely chopped walnuts	125 mL

1. In a bowl, soak raisins in warm water for 10 minutes.

2. Preheat oven to 375°F (190°C).

3. Peel and grate apples. Sprinkle with lemon juice to prevent browning. Drain the raisins and combine with grated apples, lemon zest, cinnamon, cardamom and ginger.

4. Brush three sheets of phyllo dough with melted butter and stack them on top of each other. Sprinkle with half of the walnuts and top with half of the apple mixture. Repeat with three more sheets of phyllo and the remaining nuts and apples.

5. Place one stack on top of the other and transfer to prepared baking sheet. Brush the remaining three sheets with the remaining melted butter, lightly crinkle the top phyllo sheet and place on top of stack. Bake for 25 minutes or until golden.

Crêpes, Blinis and Waffles

Crêpe Batter

Makes about 3 cups (750 mL) batter

We make our crêpe batter with whole wheat flour. You can use all-purpose flour instead, or replace a fourth of the flour with chestnut flour, which gives the crêpes a delicate flavor.

Tips

How much liquid you'll need depends on the type of flour you use. For thin and tender crêpes, make sure the batter isn't too thick or too thin.

To cook crêpes, heat a crêpe pan or nonstick skillet over medium heat until hot. Pour in a little oil or butter, turning the pan to ensure that the oil spreads evenly over the entire surface. Pour a little batter into the pan with a small ladle. Rotate the pan so that the batter covers the whole surface and cook 30 to 45 seconds per side. Keep the first crêpes warm while you prepare the rest.

½	vanilla bean	½
1 cup	soy milk or skim milk	250 mL
¾ cup	whole wheat flour	175 mL
3	eggs, beaten	3
Pinch	salt	Pinch
¼ cup	water	50 mL
1 tbsp	butter, melted	15 mL

1. Split the vanilla bean in half, scrape out the seeds and let them steep in the milk for 15 minutes.

2. In a large bowl, combine flour, eggs and salt. Gradually add milk mixture, stirring constantly. When all the milk is incorporated, stir in water.

3. Pour melted butter over batter, cover and let stand at room temperature for at least 2 hours or refrigerate for up to 1 day. When ready to use, let warm to room temperature, if necessary, and thin with a little water as necessary.

Crêpes with Ricotta Cheese, Nuts and Bananas

Serves 6

These crêpes trace their origins to Brittany. In this region of France, the soil is too poor to cultivate wheat, so the population traditionally consumed crêpes instead of bread. We make our batter with whole wheat flour. But you can replace it with all-purpose flour or 30% chestnut flour, which gives the crêpes a refined flavor.

Tips

How much liquid you'll need depends on the type of flour you use. For thin and tender crêpes, make sure the batter isn't too thick or too thin. For ultra-thin crêpes, beat an egg white until firm and add it to the batter just before cooking.

A plate of freshly prepared crêpes can also be accompanied by applesauce, prune paste, pear filling or ground cinnamon.

½	vanilla bean	½
½ cup	soy milk or skim milk	125 mL
⅓ cup	whole wheat flour	75 mL
2	eggs, beaten	2
Pinch	salt	Pinch
2 tbsp	water	25 mL
2 tsp	butter, melted	10 mL
	Vegetable oil	
2	bananas, sliced	2
¾ cup	ricotta cheese	175 mL
½ cup	toasted ground almonds	125 mL

1. Split the vanilla bean in half, scrape out the seeds and let them steep in the milk for 15 minutes.

2. In a large bowl, combine flour, eggs and salt. Gradually add milk mixture, stirring constantly. When all the milk is incorporated, stir in water.

3. Pour melted butter over batter, cover and let stand at room temperature for 2 hours or refrigerate for up to 1 day. When ready to use, let warm to room temperature, if necessary, and thin with a little water as necessary.

4. Heat a skillet over medium heat until hot. Pour in a little oil, turning the pan to ensure that the oil spreads evenly over the entire surface. Pour a little batter into the pan with a small ladle. Rotate the pan so that the batter covers the whole surface and cook for 30 to 45 seconds per side. Keep the first crêpes warm while you prepare the rest.

5. Heat bananas slightly in the microwave or under the broiler. Place crêpes on the table, along with bananas, ricotta cheese and almonds, and let diners prepare their own crêpes.

Whole Wheat Flour Crêpes with Ricotta Cheese and Raspberry Sauce

Serves 4		

If you cook these crêpes four at a time in a large skillet, you'll have a delicious snack in just a few minutes. These crêpes are also an excellent way to start the day. Perfect for Sunday brunch!

Tips

Blending ricotta cheese into the batter makes these crêpes lighter and airier.

You can also serve them with applesauce, puréed pears or other fruits of your choice.

Sauce

2½ cups	raspberries, divided	625 mL

Crêpes

2	eggs, separated	2
1 cup	ricotta cheese	250 mL
⅔ cup	whole wheat flour	150 mL
¾ tsp	baking powder	3 mL
Pinch	salt	Pinch
3 tbsp	soy milk or skim milk	45 mL
2 tbsp	butter, melted, or vegetable oil	30 mL
	Sour cream or ricotta cheese	

1. *Prepare the sauce:* In a blender, purée half the raspberries. Transfer to a bowl and stir in the remaining raspberries. Cover and refrigerate.

2. *Prepare the crêpes:* In a bowl, combine egg yolks and ricotta cheese. Stir in flour, baking powder and salt.

3. In another bowl, beat egg whites until stiff peaks form. Fold into batter by gently lifting and turning. Stir in milk. The batter should be thick enough to coat the back of a spoon.

4. Place a large skillet over medium heat and grease well with butter. When the pan is hot, use a small ladle to pour in three or four small crêpes (depending on the size of your skillet). Spread them out slightly with the back of a wooden spoon and cook for 1 to 2 minutes per side or until golden. Remove to a plate and keep warm. Repeat with remaining batter.

5. Serve crêpes with cold raspberry sauce and a little sour cream or ricotta cheese.

Coconut Crêpes

Makes 8 crêpes

In South Asia, particularly in Thailand, street vendors serve up these ultra-light crêpes. Made with a mixture of wheat and rice flours, they are simply delicious.

Tip
Serve with ricotta cheese or a little agave syrup for the filling.

¾ cup	unsweetened shredded coconut	175 mL
½ cup	whole wheat flour	125 mL
¼ cup	rice flour	50 mL
1	egg, beaten	1
1½ cups	coconut milk	375 mL
1½ tbsp	xylitol or liquid honey OR	22 mL
1 tbsp	agave syrup	15 mL
	Vegetable oil	

1. In a large bowl, combine coconut, whole wheat flour and rice flour. Form a well in the center and add the egg. While stirring, add coconut milk and the natural sugar of your choice and continue stirring to obtain a smooth batter.

2. Heat a large skillet over medium heat until hot, then brush with oil. Use a small ladle to pour in three or four small crêpes. Spread them out slightly with the back of a wooden spoon and cook for 1 minute per side or until golden. Remove to a plate and keep warm. Repeat with the remaining batter.

Crêpes "Aumônières" with Prunes

The key to these unique crêpes is starting off right: a light batter, enhanced by an egg white that has been beaten until stiff peaks form. Next, the crêpes must be poured quite thin and cooked over low heat to ensure they remain soft and supple.

Tip
Be sure to use ripe bananas for the best flavor.

24	large prunes	24
1	vanilla bean, split	1
Pinch	ground cinnamon	Pinch
1	egg white	1
1	recipe Crêpe Batter (page 60)	1
	Vegetable oil	
2	bananas	2
	Grated zest of 1 orange	
12	strips of orange peel	12

1. Place prunes in a bowl, cover with warm water and let soak for 25 minutes.

2. Transfer prunes to a saucepan and add vanilla bean and cinnamon. Bring to a simmer over medium heat. Reduce heat and simmer, stirring occasionally, for 30 minutes. Let cool.

3. In a bowl, beat egg white until stiff peaks form. Fold into crêpe batter by gently lifting and turning (this makes the crêpes softer and more flexible). If the batter is too thick, add a little water so the crêpes will come out thin with a soft texture.

4. Heat a skillet over medium heat until hot. Pour in a little oil, turning the pan to ensure that the oil spreads evenly over the entire surface. Pour a little batter into the pan with a small ladle. Rotate the pan so that the batter covers the whole surface and cook for 30 to 45 seconds per side. Keep the first crêpes warm while you prepare the rest.

5. Drain prunes, reserving some of the juice, and remove the pits, being careful not to damage the fruit.

Tip

We like to serve these crêpes warm, accompanied by a cool sorbet.

6. Slice bananas and purée in a blender. Stir in orange zest and a little of the reserved prune juice.

7. Spoon some banana purée onto each crêpe. Place 2 prunes in the center. Bring the edge of the crêpe together to meet at the top, hold the crêpe closed with one hand and place a strip of orange peel like a latch to maintain the closure. Serve warm.

Raspberry Crêpes

Makes 4 large crêpes

These crêpes are made with both corn flour and quinoa flour. If you have difficulty finding quinoa flour, you may substitute rice flour.

Tips

Vary the fruits — why not try these crêpes with a filling made from fresh figs?

If stevia is available as a sweetener in your area, you can use it in this recipe by dissolving $\frac{1}{8}$ tsp (0.5 mL) stevia extract powder (or the equivalent of 2 tbsp/ 25 mL sugar) in 2 tbsp (25 mL) extra water and adding it with the soy milk.

Sauce

1 $\frac{1}{4}$ cups	raspberries	300 mL
1 tbsp	lemon juice	15 mL
1 tbsp	water	15 mL

Crêpes

$\frac{1}{4}$ cup	corn flour	50 mL
$\frac{1}{4}$ cup	quinoa flour	50 mL
1	egg, beaten	1
1 cup	soy milk or skim milk	250 mL
2$\frac{1}{2}$ tbsp	water	32 mL
2 tbsp	xylitol or honey OR	25 mL
4 tsp	agave syrup	20 mL
	Vegetable oil	

1. *Prepare the sauce:* In a small saucepan, combine raspberries, lemon juice and water. Heat over low heat for about 10 minutes.

2. *Meanwhile, prepare the crêpes:* In a large bowl, combine corn flour and quinoa flour. Form a well in the center and add the egg. While stirring, add milk, water and the natural sugar of your choice and continue stirring to obtain a smooth batter.

3. Heat a skillet over medium heat until hot. Pour in a little oil, turning the pan to ensure that the oil spreads evenly over the entire surface. Pour a little batter into the pan with a small ladle. Rotate the pan so that the batter covers the whole surface and cook for 30 to 45 seconds per side or until golden. Remove to a plate and keep warm. Repeat with the remaining batter.

4. Spoon a little raspberry sauce onto the center of each crêpe, fold and serve.

Chocolate Crêpes with Pistachios

I love to prepare these crêpes for an energetic breakfast. I start the night before with an oatmeal base that I soak in orange juice for a wonderful flavor.

Tip

Toast the pistachio nuts before chopping and they will taste even better.

1 cup	large-flake (old-fashioned) rolled oats	250 mL
½ cup	freshly squeezed orange juice	125 mL
	Hazelnut oil	
1	egg, beaten	1
2 tbsp	unsweetened cocoa powder	25 mL
2 tbsp	xylitol or liquid honey	25 mL
3 tbsp	coconut milk or soy milk (approx.)	45 mL
2 tbsp	unsalted pistachios, coarsely chopped	25 mL

1. In a bowl, combine oats with orange juice. Cover and refrigerate overnight.

2. In a skillet, heat a thin layer of hazelnut oil over medium. Mix egg into oat mixture. Spoon into skillet, forming two crêpes, and cook for 2 to 3 minutes per side or until golden. Remove to a plate and keep warm.

3. In a small double boiler, combine cocoa, the natural sugar of your choice and coconut milk. Heat over low heat, whisking, until melted into smooth chocolate sauce. Add more milk if needed to reach the right consistency.

4. Spread the sauce over the crêpes and sprinkle with pistachios.

Chestnut and Chocolate Crêpes Napoleon

I envisioned this cake one windy and rainy Sunday afternoon as winter drew near. The bad weather reminded me of Vienna and its famous Sacher Café, where I savored an espresso-flavored chocolate-almond cake one brisk autumn day. I had no idea what their recipe was, so I improvised with what I found at home in my kitchen. The experiment turned out to be an absolute delight, a cake both easy to prepare and economical.

• • ◆ • •

Tip

If preparing the cake for children, replace the espresso with partly skimmed milk.

1	recipe Crêpe Batter (page 60), prepared with ½ cup (125 mL) all-purpose flour and ¼ cup (50 mL) chestnut flour	1
1	can or jar (15 oz/425 g) roasted chestnuts	1
½ cup	unsweetened cocoa powder	125 mL
¼ cup	strong brewed espresso	50 mL
¼ cup	liquid honey OR	50 mL
3 tbsp	agave syrup	45 mL
1 tbsp	butter	15 mL
1 tbsp	ground cinnamon	15 mL
3 tbsp	sliced almonds, lightly toasted	45 mL

1. Heat a large skillet over medium heat until hot. Pour in a little oil, turning the pan to ensure that the oil spreads evenly over the entire surface. Pour a little batter into the pan with a small ladle. Rotate the pan so that the batter covers the whole surface and cook for 40 to 60 seconds per side or until golden. Remove to a plate and keep warm. Repeat with the remaining batter, making 6 crêpes in total. Set aside.

2. In a blender, purée the chestnuts and set aside.

3. In a small double boiler, combine cocoa, espresso and the natural sugar of your choice. Melt over low heat. Blend in butter, then remove from heat and let cool slightly. Whisk in chestnut purée and cinnamon.

4. Stack 2 crêpes on a large plate. Spread chestnut and chocolate filling over the top crêpe. Repeat the layers twice more, ending with a layer of filling. Pack down into a firm cake. Sprinkle almonds on top of cake. Cover loosely and refrigerate for at least 2 hours or for up to 1 day. Slice into wedges to serve.

Buckwheat Flour Blinis with Smothered Apple Slices

We had the idea for this recipe while tasting buckwheat flour blinis in the most charming crêperie in Brittany, somewhere up on the wild coast. These blinis, so simple and quick to prepare, very pleasantly accompany tea or coffee in the afternoon.

Variation
You can substitute banana or pear slices for the apple slices. A most unexpected, but no less delicious variation features small pineapple wedges.

6 tbsp	soy milk or skim milk	90 mL
2 tbsp	butter, divided	25 mL
1	medium egg, separated	1
⅓ cup	buckwheat or whole wheat flour	75 mL
1	sweet apple, peeled and thinly sliced	1
¼ tsp	ground cinnamon	1 mL

1. In a saucepan, warm the milk and half the butter over medium heat until butter is melted. Remove from the heat and set aside.

2. In a bowl, beat egg white until stiff peaks form.

3. Place buckwheat flour in another bowl. Make a small well in the center and add the egg yolk. Gradually pour the milk mixture into the well, mixing thoroughly to obtain a smooth batter. Fold in egg white, lightening the mixture.

4. Heat a medium skillet over medium heat. Add the remaining butter, spreading to coat pan. Pour in 4 small ladles of batter to form 4 blinis. Place a few apple slices on each so they will be smothered in the cooking batter. Lightly sprinkle with ground cinnamon. Cook for 1 to 2 minutes per side or until golden. Remove to a plate and keep warm. Repeat with the remaining batter and apples.

Whole Wheat Waffles

*During the Middle
Ages, waffles came
after dessert was served
to end a festive meal
with a flourish. Special
irons were used to give
them different forms
and shapes. This type
of waffles, often sold
on the street by mobile
vendors, were made
from a base of barley
and oats.*

Tip
These waffles are
delicious on their own,
but you can always dress
them up a bit with yogurt,
sour cream or a berry
sauce.

- *Waffle iron*

1 tbsp	light cream	15 mL
1 cup	milk, divided	250 mL
Pinch	salt	Pinch
½ cup	whole wheat flour	125 mL
2 tbsp	butter	25 mL
3	eggs	3

1. In a saucepan, combine cream and half the milk. Bring to a boil over medium heat. Remove from heat.

2. In another saucepan, combine the remaining milk and salt. Bring to a boil over medium heat. Gradually add flour, stirring constantly. Add butter, stirring constantly. Cook, stirring constantly, for 2 to 3 minutes until dough comes away from the sides of the pan.

3. Pour into a large bowl and beat in eggs, one at a time. Stir in the boiled cream mixture. Let cool.

4. Meanwhile, preheat waffle iron.

5. Cook waffles according to manufacturer's instructions, keeping cooked waffles warm while preparing the rest.

French Toast with Apples

In Quebec, French toast is called quite rightly "golden bread." For this ancestral recipe, we use organic whole wheat bread and remove the crusts. We then grill it before letting it soak in the egg-milk mixture. If you like, sprinkle this dessert with fruit sauce or agave syrup. Be careful measuring out agave syrup, as it is sweeter than refined sugar.

Tip

Always choose fruit of a sweet variety that holds together when cooked.

Variation

Also try this dessert with pears.

• **Preheat broiler (optional)**

2 cups	milk	500 mL
	Grated zest of 1 lemon	
1 ½ tsp	ground cinnamon	7 mL
4	eggs, beaten	4
8	slices organic whole wheat bread, crusts removed	8
1 tsp	light butter	5 mL
2	apples, peeled and cut into wedges	2
2 tbsp	nut oil	25 mL

1. In a saucepan, combine milk, lemon zest and cinnamon over medium heat until steaming. Let cool and pour into a shallow dish. Stir in eggs.

2. Toast bread on both sides in the toaster or under the broiler. Soak toast in the milk mixture, letting them saturate well but not too much, so they keep their shape.

3. Meanwhile, in a skillet, melt butter over medium heat. Sauté apples for about 5 minutes or until golden. Remove from heat and set aside.

4. In a large skillet, heat the nut oil over medium heat. Drain the bread and, working in batches, brown gently on both sides. Remove to a plate lined with paper towels to drain. Keep warm while cooking the rest.

5. Place French toast on a large dish and decorate with apple segments. Serve hot.

Chocolate Banana Croque

	Serves 4	

You surely know the classic croque-monsieur, a French invention dating from the beginning of the 20th century. The famous author Marcel Proust mentions it in his work In the Shadow of Young Girls in Flower, *published in 1919: "While going out of the concert, upon resuming our route back to the hotel, we stopped a moment on the sea wall, my grandmother and I, to exchange a few words with Madame de Villeparisis, who announced she had ordered waiting for us at the hotel croque-monsieur and eggs with cream ..." Here is a dessert version — a delicious croque, quick and easy to prepare.*

• • ◆ • •

Tip

For the best results, use an appliance for toasted sandwiches, like a croque-monsieur maker or panini press, if you have one available.

8	thick slices white sandwich bread	8
¼ cup	butter, softened	50 mL
2	small bananas, mashed	2
5 oz	chocolate, broken into pieces	150 g
4 tsp	powdered or desiccated unsweetened coconut (optional)	20 mL

1. Butter each slice of bread on one side. Place four of the slices on a plate, buttered side down. Spread each with a little mashed banana and place chocolate pieces over top. Sprinkle with coconut (if using). Cover with the remaining slices of bread, buttered side up.

2. Heat a nonstick skillet over medium heat. Working in batches as necessary, cook sandwiches for about 4 minutes per side or until golden brown. Serve hot.

Muffins, Scones and Breads

Apple-Blueberry Muffins

Muffins are always popular with kids, and countless variations are possible. Here, apples and blueberries go very well together.

Tips

As with scones, muffins are best eaten the day they are made. If there are any left over, freeze them and defrost in the microwave whenever you need them.

In the muffin batter, you can also use ¼ cup (50 mL) agave syrup instead of the xylitol or honey.

If stevia is available as a sweetener in your area, you can use it in this recipe by dissolving ¼ tsp (1 mL) stevia extract powder (or the equivalent of ⅓ cup/ 75 mL sugar) in ⅓ cup (75 mL) extra milk and adding it to the milk mixture in the muffin batter. For the topping, dissolve ⅛ tsp (0.5 mL) stevia extract powder (or the equivalent of 2 tbsp/25 mL sugar) in 2 tbsp (25 mL) warm water and add it to the oats mixture.

- **Preheat oven to 375°F (190°C)**
- **12-cup muffin tin, buttered**

1½ cups	all-purpose flour	375 mL
1½ cups	whole wheat flour	375 mL
1 tbsp	baking powder	15 mL
1 tsp	salt	5 mL
½ tsp	ground ginger	2 mL
¼ tsp	ground cinnamon	1 mL
Pinch	ground cloves	Pinch
1 cup	soy milk or skim milk	250 mL
2	eggs	2
½ cup	melted butter	125 mL
⅓ cup	xylitol or liquid honey	75 mL
2	apples, peeled and grated	2
1⅓ cups	blueberries	325 mL

Topping

⅓ cup	large-flake rolled oats	75 mL
¼ cup	all-purpose or whole wheat flour	50 mL
2 tbsp	xylitol, liquid honey or agave syrup	25 mL
3 tbsp	butter	45 mL

1. In a bowl, combine all-purpose flour, whole wheat flour, baking powder, salt, ginger, cinnamon and cloves.

2. In another bowl, whisk milk, eggs, butter and the natural sugar of your choice. Pour over the flour mixture and stir quickly until just combined; it should be sticky and still have lumps. Fold in apples and blueberries. Divide batter evenly among prepared muffin cups.

3. *Prepare the topping:* In a bowl, combine oats, flour and the natural sugar of your choice. Using your fingers, work in butter until mixture is crumbly. Sprinkle evenly over muffins.

4. Bake in preheated oven for 25 minutes or until tops spring back when lightly pressed. Let cool in pan for a few minutes, then remove to a wire rack to cool completely.

Banana-Coconut Muffins with Figs and Cocoa

Makes 12 muffins

There are two kinds of muffins, the English muffin and the American-style muffin (or "quick bread" muffin). The English muffin, invented in the 11th century, is made with baker's yeast, while the American variety, a spinoff of cake, is made with baking powder. Either way, muffins are excellent filled with ingredients such as berries, pecans or bananas.

Tips

If self-rising cake flour isn't available, substitute 2 cups (500 mL) cake flour or cake-and-pastry flour, 1 tbsp (15 mL) baking powder and 1 tsp (5 mL) salt.

If stevia is available as a sweetener in your area, you can use it in this recipe by dissolving $\frac{1}{8}$ tsp (0.5 mL) stevia extract powder (or the equivalent of 2 tbsp/ 25 mL sugar) in 2 tbsp (25 mL) extra yogurt or water and adding it with the yogurt.

• *Preheat oven to 400°F (200°C)*
• *12-cup muffin tin or individual molds, buttered*

2 cups	self-rising cake flour (see tip, at left)	500 mL
$\frac{1}{4}$ cup	high-quality unsweetened cocoa powder	50 mL
2 tbsp	unsweetened shredded coconut, divided	25 mL
1 tsp	spice blend of ground ginger, cinnamon and cardamom	5 mL
Pinch	salt	Pinch
3	eggs	3
2	large ripe bananas, mashed	2
$\frac{1}{3}$ cup	hazelnut or sesame oil	75 mL
$\frac{1}{3}$ cup	plain yogurt	75 mL
2 tbsp	xylitol or liquid honey OR	25 mL
4 tsp	agave syrup	20 mL
$\frac{3}{4}$ cup	diced dried figs	175 mL

1. In a bowl, combine flour, cocoa, 4 tsp (20 mL) of the coconut, spice blend and salt.

2. In another bowl, whisk together eggs, bananas, hazelnut oil, yogurt and the natural sugar of your choice. Pour over the flour mixture and stir quickly until just combined; it should be sticky and still have lumps. Fold in figs. Divide batter evenly among prepared muffin cups. Sprinkle tops with the remaining coconut.

3. Bake in preheated oven for 20 to 25 minutes or until tops spring back when lightly pressed. Let cool in pan for a few minutes, then remove to a wire rack to cool completely.

Date Muffins

Muffins are fast and easy to make. Since they take only a few minutes, they're ideal for a spur-of-the-moment afternoon snack. Do not overmix the batter; it should be slightly lumpy.

Tip

We use a 12-cup muffin tin to make our muffins. You can also use small paper baking molds or a silicone muffin pan; there's no need to butter paper molds or a silicone pan, so the muffins will have fewer calories.

- *Preheat oven to 350°F (180°C)*
- *12-cup muffin tin, buttered*

1 cup	water	250 mL
1¼ cups	chopped pitted dates	300 mL
2 tsp	baking soda, divided	10 mL
1 cup	whole wheat flour	250 mL
1 cup	all-purpose flour	250 mL
1½ tsp	baking powder	7 mL
½ tsp	salt	2 mL
2	eggs	2
⅓ cup	butter, softened	75 mL
1 cup	chopped walnuts	250 mL

1. In a saucepan, bring water, dates and 1 tsp (5 mL) of the baking soda to a boil over high heat. Remove from heat and let cool.

2. In a bowl, combine whole wheat flour, all-purpose flour, the remaining baking soda, baking powder and salt.

3. In another bowl, using an electric mixer, cream eggs and butter until light and fluffy. Gradually add the flour mixture, stirring briskly after each addition. Fold in the date mixture and walnuts. Divide batter evenly among prepared muffin cups.

4. Bake in preheated oven for 25 to 30 minutes or until tops spring back when lightly pressed. Let cool in pan for a few minutes, then remove to a wire rack to cool completely.

Oatmeal-Fig Muffins

We originally made these muffins with oat flour, but they are just as delicious with oatmeal, which is easier to find in stores. Try them for breakfast or for an afternoon snack while still warm; topped with ricotta or fromage blanc, they're delightful!

Tip

Oats have a very low glycemic index compared to other grains, which makes them more effective at reducing bad cholesterol.

- *Preheat oven to 400°F (200°C)*
- *12-cup muffin tin, 8 cups buttered*

1²⁄₃ cups	all-purpose flour	400 mL
1 cup	large-flake (old-fashioned) rolled oats	250 mL
¹⁄₂ cup	raisins	125 mL
4¹⁄₂ tsp	baking powder	22 mL
³⁄₄ tsp	salt	3 mL
¹⁄₂ tsp	ground cinnamon	2 mL
¹⁄₃ cup	dried figs	75 mL
1 cup	milk (approx.)	250 mL
2	eggs	2
¹⁄₄ cup	hazelnut or sesame oil	50 mL

1. In a large bowl, combine flour, oats, raisins, baking powder, salt and cinnamon.

2. In a blender, purée figs with milk until smooth.

3. In another bowl, beat eggs until frothy. Whisk in oil, then the fig mixture. Pour over flour mixture and stir until combined. The batter should be fluid; if necessary, add some milk. Divide the batter evenly among the 8 prepared muffin cups.

3. Bake in preheated oven for 20 to 25 minutes or until the tops spring back when lightly pressed. Let cool in pan for a few minutes, then remove to a wire rack to cool completely.

Light Scones

Scones are a great classic in British pastry-making. They generally include dates, raisins or currants. Devonshire scones, served as part of an afternoon tea with clotted cream and jam, are renowned. Scones, which are very quick to make, are best eaten the day they are baked.

Tip
If there are any leftover scones, freeze them and reheat them as needed.

- *Preheat oven to 425°F (220°C)*
- *2-inch (5 cm) fluted biscuit cutter, floured*
- *2 baking sheets, buttered and lightly dusted with flour*

1²⁄₃ cups	cake flour	400 mL
1¹⁄₃ cups	whole wheat flour	325 mL
2 tbsp	baking powder	25 mL
½ tsp	salt	2 mL
⅓ cup	light butter, softened	75 mL
⅓ cup	raisins	75 mL
2	eggs	2
1 cup	milk	250 mL
	Butter, clotted cream or sugar-free organic jam	

1. In a bowl, combine cake flour, whole wheat flour, baking powder and salt. Work in butter with your fingers until the dough resembles coarse crumbs. Fold in raisins.

2. In another bowl, beat eggs. Gradually stir in milk, then pour over the flour mixture. Working quickly, using a fork, blend until dough is sticky and damp. Do not overmix.

3. Turn dough out onto a very lightly floured work surface and pat out to ¾-inch (2 cm) thickness. Using the floured biscuit cutter, cut out scones and place on prepared baking sheets, rerolling scraps once.

4. Bake in preheated oven for 10 to 15 minutes or until puffed and golden. Serve warm, split in half, with a little butter, clotted cream or sugar-free organic jam.

Apricot and Raisin Scones

Makes 8 scones

Scones are British snacks of Scottish origin. A small quick bread made of wheat, barley or oatmeal, usually with baking powder as a leavening agent, the scone is a basic component of Devonshire tea, or cream tea. According to the Oxford English Dictionary, the word "scone" may derive from the Middle Dutch schoonbrood (fine white bread).

Tips

Cut the scones in half and spread with jam, honey, butter or honey.

You may also flavor the flour with 1 tsp (5 mL) ground cinnamon.

- **Preheat oven to 400°F (200°C)**
- **3-inch (7.5 cm) biscuit cutter, coffee cup or glass, floured**
- **Nonstick baking sheet**

3¼ cups	all-purpose flour	800 mL
2 tbsp	baking powder	25 mL
1½ tsp	salt	7 mL
2 tbsp	xylitol or liquid honey	25 mL
¾ cup	butter, softened, cut in cubes	175 mL
2	eggs	2
¾ cup	milk	175 mL
10	dried apricots, diced	10
½ cup	raisins	125 mL
1	egg yolk, whisked with 1 tsp (5 mL) water	1

1. In a bowl, combine flour, baking powder and salt. Stir in the natural sugar of your choice. Work in butter with your fingers until the dough resembles coarse crumbs.

2. In another bowl, beat eggs. Gradually stir in milk, then pour over the flour mixture. Working quickly, using a fork, blend until dough is sticky and damp. Do not overmix. Add apricots and raisins; knead lightly until incorporated.

3. Turn dough out onto a floured work surface and pat out to 1½-inch (4 cm) thickness. Using the floured biscuit cutter, cut out scones and place on baking sheet, rerolling scraps. Brush scones with egg wash.

4. Bake in preheated oven for 15 to 20 minutes or until puffed and golden. Serve warm or let scones cool and store in an airtight container.

Scottish Potato Scones

These scones are very popular in Scotland. To make them healthier, we make them with small new potatoes (just scrub their skins) and whole wheat flour.

Tip
These scones can be eaten immediately while still hot or the next day. Serve them with ricotta or fromage blanc.

8 oz	new potatoes (about 4 small)	250 g
2 tbsp	light butter	25 mL
¼ cup	whole wheat flour	50 mL
¼ tsp	salt	1 mL
¼ tsp	baking powder	1 mL
	Sunflower or sesame oil	

1. Scrub potatoes under running water but don't peel them. Place potatoes in a saucepan, cover with cold water and bring to a boil over high heat. Reduce heat and boil gently for about 15 minutes or until tender.

2. Drain potatoes and return to the pan. Add butter and mash until no lumps remain. Measure 1 cup (250 mL) of mashed potatoes for the scones, reserving any extra for another use.

3. In a bowl, combine mashed potatoes, flour, salt and baking powder; mix until dough is pliable.

4. Turn dough out onto a lightly floured work surface. With floured hands, pat out to a square about ¼ inch (0.5 cm) thick. Cut into 8 small squares. Brush all sides with oil.

5. Heat a skillet over medium heat until hot. Cook scones, turning carefully, for 3 to 4 minutes per side or until golden brown.

"Mozartissimo" Kugelhopf

Kugelhopf is a type of brioche from Alsace, and is very popular in Germany, Austria and neighboring countries. In Vienna, it is flavored with fresh tarragon, which gives it a delicate but surprising flavor!

Tip
This kugelhopf keeps for several days, wrapped and kept cool. You can also grill it before eating. It's excellent!

- *Preheat oven to 350°F (180°C)*
- *8-cup (2 L) kugelhopf dish, buttered and lightly floured*

¼ cup	raisins	50 mL
	Hot water	
1⅔ cups	sifted all-purpose flour	400 mL
1½ tsp	baking powder	7 mL
Pinch	salt	Pinch
⅔ cup	butter, softened	150 mL
2	eggs	2
3	ripe bananas, puréed	3
Pinch	ground ginger	Pinch
Pinch	ground nutmeg	Pinch
¾ cup	roughly chopped pecans	175 mL

1. In a bowl, soak raisins in hot water for 5 minutes. Drain well.

2. In another bowl, combine flour, baking powder and salt.

3. In a large bowl, using an electric mixer, beat butter and eggs until light and fluffy. Beat in bananas, ginger and nutmeg. Stir in drained raisins. Fold in flour mixture and pecans until incorporated. Pour into prepared dish.

4. Bake in preheated oven for about 1 hour or until a tester inserted in the center comes out clean. Let cool in dish on a wire rack for 10 minutes, then turn out onto rack to cool completely.

Chocolate and Dried Fruit Croissants

These pastries are so delicious that they disappear as soon as they're made! We've never been able to wait to let them cool down ...

Tips

We rinse and drain all dried fruit before use.

If stevia is available as a sweetener in your area, you can use it in this recipe by dissolving ⅛ tsp (0.5 mL) stevia extract powder (or the equivalent of 2 tbsp/ 25 mL sugar) in 2 tbsp (25 mL) extra soy milk or milk and adding it to the cocoa mixture.

• **2 baking sheets, lined with parchment paper**

Pastry

1	egg, separated	1
¾ cup	low-fat fromage frais (unripened fresh cheese)	175 mL
3 tbsp	soy milk or skim milk	45 mL
⅔ cup	all-purpose flour	150 mL
⅔ cup	whole wheat flour	150 mL
1 tbsp	baking powder	15 mL
1 tsp	salt	5 mL

Filling

¾ cup	unsweetened cocoa powder	175 mL
Pinch	ground cinnamon	Pinch
Pinch	ground ginger, cardamom or cloves (or a blend)	Pinch
2 tbsp	liquid honey or xylitol OR	25 mL
4 tsp	agave syrup	20 mL
1 tbsp	soy milk or skim milk	15 mL
½ cup	chopped dried apricots	125 mL
⅓ cup	raisins	75 mL
¼ cup	chopped dried figs	50 mL
½ tsp	grated lemon zest	2 mL

1. *Prepare the pastry:* In a bowl, combine egg yolk, fromage frais and milk. Stir in all-purpose flour, whole wheat flour, baking powder and salt, mixing until a soft dough forms. Cover with plastic wrap and refrigerate for 2 hours.

Variation

You can make apple turnovers using the same method. Replace the chocolate filling with an apple compote.

2. *Prepare the filling:* Meanwhile, in a heatproof bowl or the top of a double boiler, combine cocoa, cinnamon, ginger, the natural sugar of your choice and milk. Heat over simmering water, stirring until blended and smooth. Stir in apricots, raisins, figs and lemon zest. Let cool completely.

3. Preheat oven to 350°F (180°C).

4. Turn dough out onto a floured work surface and roll out to a rectangle about ¼ inch (0.5 cm) thick. Cut lengthwise into three strips.

5. Spoon one-third of the filling lengthwise in the center of each strip. Moisten the edges and roll into a sausage-like shape, pressing the edges to seal. Cut each "sausage" crosswise into 8 pieces and place on prepared baking sheets.

6. Beat egg white with 1 tbsp (15 mL) cold water until stiff. Brush tops of croissants with egg wash.

7. Bake for 15 minutes or until golden brown. Let cool slightly on baking sheets on a wire rack. Serve warm.

Toscanini Bread

Serves 6

This bread is inspired by a Tuscan recipe, traditionally made during the grape harvest, that we got to try one day on a little farm near Verona, on the hillsides in the Chianti region of Tuscany. Served with ricotta, it is wonderful as an afternoon snack or for breakfast.

Tips

If fresh yeast isn't available, substitute 2 tbsp + 2 tsp (35 mL) active dry yeast and dissolve it in $\frac{1}{4}$ cup (50 mL) warm water according to package directions.

When grapes are in season, you can replace the raisins with sweet red grapes, such as Black Muscat, and skip the soaking step.

- **Preheat oven to 350°F (180°C)**
- **8-inch (20 cm) round baking dish, buttered**

1 cup	raisins	250 mL
$\frac{3}{4}$ cup	chopped dried figs	175 mL
$1\frac{3}{4}$ oz	fresh (baker's) yeast	50 g
$1\frac{2}{3}$ cups	whole wheat flour	400 mL
$1\frac{2}{3}$ cups	all-purpose flour	400 mL
Pinch	salt	Pinch
$\frac{1}{4}$ cup	butter, softened and cut into small pieces	50 mL
$1\frac{1}{2}$ cups	chopped walnuts, divided	375 mL
1	egg, beaten	1

1. In a bowl, cover raisins and figs with warm water and let soak for 30 minutes. Drain well.

2. Dissolve yeast in 2 tbsp (25 mL) warm water.

3. In a large bowl, combine whole wheat flour, all-purpose flour and salt. Add yeast mixture and 1 cup (250 mL) warm water; stir until a dough forms.

4. Turn dough out onto a lightly floured surface and knead until smooth. Let rise for 15 minutes.

5. In another bowl, combine butter, $1\frac{1}{4}$ cups (300 mL) of the walnuts and three-quarters of the drained raisins and figs. Add to the dough and knead thoroughly for 10 to 15 minutes. The dough should be smooth and elastic.

6. Place dough in prepared baking dish and sprinkle with the remaining walnuts, raisins and figs. Let rise for 20 to 30 minutes.

7. Brush the top with beaten egg. Bake in preheated oven for 30 to 40 minutes or until golden brown and the top sounds hollow when tapped. Let cool slightly in baking dish on a wire rack. Serve warm.

Cookies, Bars and Squares

Oat Cookies

*This is our version of
the North American
classic you'll find in
most good bakeries.
These delicious treats
are very popular with
children.*

Tip
If the dough is sticky,
flour your fingers to
flatten the cookies.

• *Baking sheets, greased or lined with parchment paper
and lightly floured*

2 cups	large-flake (old-fashioned) rolled oats	500 mL
½ cup	pitted dates	125 mL
½ cup	pitted prunes	125 mL
⅓ cup	raisins	75 mL
1 ⅓ cups	whole wheat flour	425 mL
½ tsp	baking soda	2 mL
Pinch	salt	Pinch
Pinch	ground cinnamon	Pinch
Pinch	ground cloves	Pinch
3	eggs	3
¾ cup + 2 tbsp	light butter, softened	200 mL
½ cup	chopped nuts	125 mL
	Additional whole wheat flour	

1. In a bowl, combine oats and ½ cup (125 mL) water; cover and refrigerate overnight.

2. In another bowl, cover dates and prunes with warm water and let soak for 30 minutes to soften. Drain and chop; set aside.

3. Meanwhile, in a small saucepan, cover raisins with water and bring to a simmer over medium heat. Reduce heat and simmer for 3 minutes or until very soft. Drain and let cool.

4. Preheat oven to 350°F (180°C).

5. In a bowl, combine whole wheat flour, baking soda, salt, cinnamon and cloves.

● ●

Tip

The raisins, dates and prunes sweeten these cookies. Because there is no added sugar, they don't keep for long. If you don't eat them within 48 hours, freeze them.

6. In a large bowl, using an electric mixer, beat eggs, butter and cooled raisins until well blended and creamy. Stir in the soaked oats and the flour mixture until blended. Stir in dates, prunes and nuts.

7. Drop dough by tablespoons (15 mL) at least 2 inches (5 cm) apart on prepared baking sheets and flatten dough slightly. Sprinkle lightly with flour.

8. Bake, one sheet at a time, for 10 to 12 minutes or until firm around the edges. Let cool on sheet on a wire rack for 5 minutes, then transfer to rack to cool.

Oat and Rice Flour Cookies

*We like to prepare
these cookies and
freeze them so
we always have
homemade treats on
hand when unexpected
guests arrive. They
defrost quickly and are
delicious served with
coffee or tea.*

Tip
These cookies keep well
in an airtight container
at room temperature for
2 to 3 days. Beyond that,
freeze them.

- *Preheat oven to 350°F (180°C)*
- *Baking sheets, lined with parchment paper and lightly
  floured*

2	eggs	2
¾ cup + 2 tbsp	butter, softened	200 mL
2 tbsp	liquid honey	25 mL
1 tbsp	mixed spices (ground ginger, cinnamon and cardamom)	15 mL
1 cup	rice or corn flour	250 mL
2½ cups	large-flake (old-fashioned) rolled oats	625 mL
1 cup	chopped walnuts	250 mL
½ cup	raisins	125 mL
2 tbsp	unsweetened shredded coconut	25 mL

1. In a large bowl, using an electric mixer, beat eggs,
   butter, honey and spices until smooth and creamy.
   Beat in rice flour. Stir in oats, nuts and raisins until
   evenly blended.

2. Form dough into small cookies and place at least
   2 inches (5 cm) apart on prepared baking sheets.
   Sprinkle with coconut.

3. Bake in preheated oven, one sheet at a time, for
   12 to 15 minutes or until golden. Let cool on sheet
   on a wire rack for 5 minutes, then transfer to rack
   to cool.

Chocolate Chip Cookies

*Who doesn't like
cookies? And who
doesn't like chocolate?
No wonder the
chocolate chip cookie is
a timeless classic. Hide
these if you don't want
them to be wolfed
down before they've
had a chance to cool!*

- **Preheat oven to 350°F (180°C)**
- **Baking sheets, greased**

1¾ cups	sifted all-purpose flour	425 mL
1 tsp	baking powder	5 mL
½ tsp	salt	2 mL
⅓ cup	butter, softened	75 mL
⅓ cup	xylitol or liquid honey OR	75 mL
¼ cup	agave syrup	50 mL
1	egg	1
1 tbsp	milk or soy milk	15 mL
1 cup	chopped chocolate	250 mL
⅓ cup	chopped walnuts or pecans	75 mL
¼ cup	raisins	50 mL

1. In a bowl, combine flour, baking powder and salt.

2. In a large bowl, using an electric mixer, beat butter and the natural sugar of your choice until light and airy. Beat in egg and milk. Stir in flour mixture until blended. Stir in chocolate, nuts and raisins.

3. Place spoonfuls of dough at least 2 inches (5 cm) apart on prepared baking sheets.

4. Bake in preheated oven, one sheet at a time, for 12 minutes or until firm and golden. Let cool on sheet on a wire rack for 5 minutes, then transfer to rack to cool.

Little Prince Cookies Filled with Chocolate and Figs

Makes 12 cookies

Cookies are always a great success with children, big or small. This recipe is so good that our cookies are always gobbled up well before they have time to cool.

Tip
Play with the proportions in the spice blend until you find a combination you like.

- *Preheat oven to 375°F (190°C)*
- *Baking sheets, lined with parchment paper*

Dough

¼ cup	sultana raisins	50 mL
	Grated zest of 1 orange	
1 cup	ground almonds	250 mL
¾ cup	whole wheat flour	175 mL
1½ tsp	ground cinnamon	7 mL
1½ tsp	mixed spices (ground cardamom, cloves and ginger)	7 mL
2 tbsp	liquid honey (optional)	25 mL
½ cup	soy milk or skim milk	125 mL
	Additional whole wheat flour	

Filling

2 tbsp	unsweetened cocoa powder	25 mL
¼ cup	mascarpone cheese	50 mL
4 tsp	soy milk or skim milk, warmed	20 mL
½ cup	finely chopped pitted dates	125 mL
⅓ cup	finely chopped dried figs	75 mL
2 tbsp	finely chopped dried apricots	25 mL

1. *Prepare the dough:* In a bowl, cover raisins with warm water and let soak for 15 minutes. Drain and transfer to a large bowl. Stir in orange zest, almonds, flour, cinnamon and spices, mixing thoroughly. Stir in honey (if using). Gradually stir in milk until dough is well blended and firm.

2. Shape dough into 24 small balls and place at least 2 inches (5 cm) apart on prepared baking sheets. Flatten the balls with the palm of your hand, without being too firm. Sprinkle with a little flour.

Tip

If you want to store these cookies, freeze them in an airtight container. Cookies made without sugar do not keep well at room temperature, but they do freeze well.

3. Bake in preheated oven, one sheet at a time, for 15 minutes or until golden brown. Transfer cookies to a wire rack and let cool completely.

4. *Meanwhile, prepare the filling:* In a bowl, combine cocoa, mascarpone and soy milk, stirring until cocoa is dissolved. Stir in dates, figs and apricots.

5. Spread filling on the bottom of 12 of the cookies, then sandwich each with another cookie.

Quinoa and Almond Shortbread

● ●

Makes 4 pieces

Shortbread, a typical Scottish and Danish cookie, generally contains a lot of sugar and butter. Our version, made with quinoa and almonds, is much lighter, so you can enjoy these cookies without feeling guilty!

Tips

For a prettier presentation, make a decorative pattern on top before sprinkling with almonds.

In Scotland, shortbread is traditionally broken into quarters once cooled, instead of being cut with a knife.

Shortbread will keep for 3 days in an airtight container at room temperature.

If stevia is available as a sweetener in your area, you can use it in this recipe by combining a pinch of stevia extract powder (or the equivalent of 1 tbsp/15 mL sugar) with the butter.

- *Preheat oven to 325°F (160°C)*
- *Baking sheet, lined with parchment paper*

2 tbsp	light butter, softened	25 mL
1 tbsp	xylitol	15 mL
	OR	
2 tsp	agave syrup	10 mL
¼ cup	ground almonds	50 mL
¼ cup	quinoa flour	50 mL
¼ cup	slivered almonds	50 mL

1. In a bowl, using an electric mixer or a wooden spoon, cream butter and the natural sugar of your choice. Stir in ground almonds and quinoa flour, mixing until the dough comes together but is still crumbly.

2. Turn dough out onto a very lightly floured work surface and pat into a rectangle or square no more than ½ inch (1 cm) thick. Place on prepared baking sheet and sprinkle with slivered almonds, pressing gently.

3. Bake in preheated oven for 20 minutes or until firm. Let cool completely on sheet on a wire rack, then break or cut into quarters.

Healthy Almond Macaroons

These macaroons contain hardly any carbohydrates because they are made of almond powder and egg whites. Store them in a ventilated container so they don't soften.

Tips

To make sure the egg whites are firm enough, turn the bowl over — they should stay in place. (Otherwise, of course, quickly turn the bowl back over before the egg whites fall to the floor!)

When folding egg whites into another mixture, always fold from the bottom of the bowl so as not to deflate the whites.

- *Preheat oven to 350°F (180°C)*
- *Baking sheet, lined with parchment paper*

1 cup	ground almonds	250 mL
2 tbsp	liquid honey	25 mL
1 tsp	ground ginger	5 mL
2	egg whites, at room temperature	2
18	slivered almonds	18

1. In a large bowl, combine ground almonds, honey and ginger.

2. In another bowl, using an electric mixer, beat egg whites until firm, but not dry peaks form. Fold one-quarter of the egg whites into the almond mixture. Fold in the remaining egg whites.

3. Drop by tablespoons (15 mL) onto prepared baking sheet. Gently press a slivered almond into each macaroon.

4. Bake in preheated oven for 15 to 20 minutes or until firm. Let cool completely on sheets on a wire rack. Once cool, peel off parchment paper.

Coconut-Chocolate Rochers

**Makes about
30 rochers**

*Rochers are chocolate
candies made of dark
or milk chocolate,
usually mixed with
crushed nuts. In our
recipe, we've replaced
the nuts with shredded
coconut.*

Variation
Sprinkle the still-hot
rochers with a little
shredded coconut.

- *Preheat oven to 350°F (180°C)*
- *Baking sheets, buttered*
- *Baking sheets, lined with parchment paper*

Rochers

1	egg	1
1/2 cup	xylitol	125 mL
1 1/2 cups	unsweetened shredded coconut	375 mL

Chocolate Coating

1/4 cup	butter, softened	50 mL
5 oz	bittersweet (dark) chocolate, chopped	150 g

1. *Prepare the rochers:* In a bowl, using an electric mixer, beat egg and xylitol until very thick and pale. Stir in coconut.

2. Using two spoons, drop about 2 tsp (10 mL) of dough at least 2 inches (5 cm) apart on buttered baking sheets.

3. Bake in preheated oven, one sheet at a time, for about 15 minutes or until firm to the touch. Let cool on sheet on a wire rack for 5 minutes, then transfer to rack to cool completely.

4. *Prepare the coating:* In a saucepan, melt butter and chocolate over low heat, stirring until smooth. Dip cooled rochers in coating, letting excess drain off. Place on parchment-lined baking sheets and let stand at room temperature until chocolate is set.

Turrón-Style Chocolate Hazelnut Candies

Serves 4

Turrón is a Spanish specialty made from honey, sugar, egg white and sliced almonds (when it comes from Alicante) or ground almonds (when it is made in Jijona). It comes in a rectangular or circular block. Our recipe is lower in fat but preserves all the flavor of a real turrón.

◆ ◆ ◆ ◆ ◆

Caution

This recipe contains a raw egg white. If you are concerned about the safety of raw eggs, use the pasteurized liquid egg white.

• **6-inch (15 cm) square baking dish or other medium-size mold, lined with parchment paper**

1/2 cup	xylitol	125 mL
	OR	
3 tbsp	agave syrup	45 mL
3 1/2 oz	unsweetened chocolate, chopped	105 g
1/2 cup	ground hazelnuts	125 mL
1	egg white (or 2 tbsp/25 mL pasteurized liquid egg white)	1

1. In a small saucepan, combine the natural sugar of your choice and 3 tbsp (45 mL) water. Cook over low heat for 10 minutes. Add chocolate and stir until a thick paste forms. Pour into a heatproof dish and let cool. Stir in hazelnuts.

2. In a bowl, using an electric mixer, beat egg white until stiff peaks form. Fold in chocolate mixture. Spread into prepared baking dish and cover with parchment paper. Refrigerate for at least 3 hours or for up to 1 day.

3. Using a knife or spoon, cut into bite-size pieces and serve chilled.

British Flapjack Fruit and Nut Bars

Flapjacks, a typical British dessert, are cookies made in a baking pan and cut into bars. We use oats in the recipe at right, but these are also delicious made with buckwheat or rice flakes, if you can find them.

Tips

Store in an airtight container at room temperature for up to 3 days; beyond that, freeze them.

If stevia is available as a sweetener in your area, you can use it in this recipe by dissolving 1/8 tsp (0.5 mL) stevia extract powder (or the equivalent of 2 tbsp/ 25 mL sugar) in 2 tbsp (25 mL) extra water and adding it with the butter.

Variations

Replace the almonds with chopped hazelnuts or pecans.

Substitute dried apricots or figs for the dates.

- **Preheat oven to 400°F (200°C)**
- **8-inch (20 cm) square baking pan**

2/3 cup	pitted dates	150 mL
1/2 cup	light butter	125 mL
2 tbsp	xylitol or liquid honey OR	25 mL
4 tsp	agave syrup	20 mL
2 1/4 cups	large-flake (old-fashioned) rolled oats	550 mL
1/2 cup	slivered almonds, lightly toasted	125 mL
1/2 cup	sunflower or sesame seeds	125 mL

1. In a small saucepan, combine dates and 1/3 cup (75 mL) water. Cook over low heat, stirring often, until liquid is absorbed. Add butter and the natural sugar of your choice and cook until the butter melts. Mix well or purée in a blender.

2. Transfer to a bowl and stir in oats, almonds and sunflower seeds. Pour into prepared baking pan and press down firmly.

3. Bake in preheated oven for 20 minutes or until browned and firm. While still hot, cut into 12 bars and let cool in pan on a wire rack.

Whole Wheat Flour Crêpes with Ricotta Cheese and Raspberry Sauce (page 62)

Chocolate and Dried Fruit Croissants (page 82)

Healthy Almond Macaroons (page 93)

Fig and Apricot Chocolate Bars (page 97), Miniature Coconut Chocolate Bars (page 98) and British Flapjack Fruit and Nut Bars (page 96)

Fig and Apricot Chocolate Bars

When testing this recipe, we originally created a tart. But when we cut it into pieces, we realized it could make delicious bars for an afternoon snack. The crust is a sweet pastry dough and the creamy filling is made from unsweetened cocoa and finely chopped dried fruit.

Tip

If stevia is available as a sweetener in your area, you can use it in this recipe by dissolving $\frac{1}{8}$ tsp (0.5 mL) stevia extract powder (or the equivalent of 2 tbsp/ 25 mL sugar) in 2 tbsp (25 mL) extra orange juice and adding it to the cocoa mixture.

- *Preheat oven to 350°F (180°C)*
- *13- by 9-inch (33 by 23 cm) baking pan, buttered*

7 oz	Pâte Sablée (see recipe, page 17)	210 g
$\frac{1}{4}$ cup	unsweetened cocoa powder	50 mL
6 tbsp	orange juice	90 mL
2 tbsp	xylitol or liquid honey OR	25 mL
4 tsp	agave syrup	20 mL
	Grated zest of 1 orange	
$\frac{1}{2}$ tsp	mixed spices (ground cloves, cinnamon and cardamom)	2 mL
$\frac{3}{4}$ cup	dried apricots	175 mL
$\frac{3}{4}$ cup	pitted dates	175 mL
$\frac{1}{2}$ cup	dried figs	125 mL
2 tbsp	hazelnut oil	25 mL
$1\frac{1}{4}$ cups	large-flake (old-fashioned) rolled oats	300 mL

1. On a floured work surface, roll out dough and fit into prepared baking pan. Prick the bottom with a fork. Bake in preheated oven for 25 to 30 minutes or until golden brown. Set aside and preheat broiler.

2. Meanwhile, in a small saucepan, combine cocoa, orange juice and the natural sugar of your choice. Cook over medium heat, stirring for a few minutes without letting it come to a boil. Stir in orange zest and spices. Remove from heat and set aside.

3. In a blender, purée apricots, dates, figs and hazelnut oil until thick and smooth. Add the cocoa mixture and blend for few more minutes. Spread over the baked crust, press down firmly and sprinkle with oats.

4. Broil for a few minutes, until oats are lightly browned. Let cool completely, then cover and refrigerate for at least 2 hours or for up to 3 days. Cut into bars when ready to serve.

Miniature Coconut Chocolate Bars

**Makes
12 mini bars**

This low-calorie version of the traditional chocolate bar can be enjoyed as a bite-size sweet with afternoon tea or coffee. Bon appétit!

- *Preheat oven to 350°F (180°C)*
- *Baking sheet, lined with parchment paper*

3	egg whites	3
2 cups	unsweetened shredded coconut	500 mL
1 tbsp	cornstarch	15 mL
1 tsp	lemon juice	5 mL
3 tbsp	unsweetened cocoa powder	45 mL
3 tbsp	soy milk	45 mL
1½ tbsp	butter	22 mL
1 tbsp	liquid honey	15 mL

1. In a bowl, whisk egg whites until frothy. Stir in coconut, cornstarch and lemon juice until well blended. Shape into 12 bars and place at least 1 inch (2.5 cm) apart on prepared baking sheet.

2. Bake in preheated oven for 10 minutes. Reduce temperature to 300°F (150°C) and bake for 5 minutes. Let cool on sheet on a wire rack.

3. In the top of a double boiler, over simmering water, combine cocoa, milk, butter and honey, stirring until melted and smooth.

4. Dip bars in chocolate sauce and place on a wire rack to cool. Return to the baking sheet and refrigerate until chocolate is set.

Coconut and Pecan Brownies

Makes 15 brownies

The brownie is thought to have been invented during the Chicago World Fair in 1893. Brownies are excellent served with ice cream or sorbet, or simply with a bit of whipped cream.

Tip

If stevia is available as a sweetener in your area, you can use it in this recipe by dissolving 1/4 tsp (1 mL) stevia extract powder (or the equivalent of 1/4 cup/ 50 mL sugar) in 3 tbsp (45 mL) extra coconut milk or soy milk and adding it to the cocoa mixture.

- *Preheat oven to 350°F (180°C)*
- *8-inch (20 cm) square baking pan, buttered and dusted with flour*

1/3 cup	unsweetened cocoa powder	75 mL
1/4 cup	butter	50 mL
2 tbsp	coconut milk or soy milk	25 mL
3 1/2 tbsp	xylitol or liquid honey OR	52 mL
2 1/2 tbsp	agave syrup	32 mL
1	egg	1
1/2 cup	finely chopped pecans	125 mL
2 1/2 tbsp	cake flour	32 mL
1 tbsp	unsweetened shredded coconut	15 mL

1. In a small saucepan, heat cocoa, butter and coconut milk over low heat until melted. Stir in the natural sugar of your choice. Remove from heat and let cool. Whisk in egg.

2. In a bowl, combine pecans and flour. Stir in the chocolate mixture until blended. Pour into prepared baking pan, smoothing the top with a spatula.

3. Bake in preheated oven for 15 to 20 minutes or until a tester inserted in the center comes out with a few moist crumbs clinging to it. Sprinkle with coconut and let cool completely in pan on a wire rack. Once cooled, cut into squares.

Dried Fruit Chocolate Brownies

Makes 12 brownies

We tried these yummy brownies in New York, where you can find them in pastry shops and fast-food joints. For our version, we use ground almonds and whole wheat flour. They're delicious served with a lemon or green apple sorbet.

Tip

If stevia is available as a sweetener in your area, you can use it in this recipe by dissolving ½ tsp (2 mL) stevia extract powder (or the equivalent of 6 tbsp/ 90 mL sugar) in 6 tbsp (25 mL) extra coconut milk and adding it to the double boiler.

- Preheat oven to 300°F (150°C)
- 8-inch (20 cm) square baking pan, lined with parchment paper

6 tbsp	xylitol or liquid honey	90 mL
	OR	
¼ cup	agave syrup	50 mL
¼ cup	coconut milk	50 mL
1 cup	unsweetened cocoa powder	250 mL
¾ cup	butter, cut into pieces	175 mL
3	eggs, beaten	3
1 ½ cups	ground almonds	375 mL
2 ½ tbsp	whole wheat flour	32 mL
½ cup	slivered almonds, toasted	125 mL
⅓ cup	chopped pitted dates	75 mL
¼ cup	chopped dried figs	50 mL

1. In the top of a double boiler, over simmering water, combine the natural sugar of your choice and coconut milk. Stir in cocoa powder and butter. Cook, stirring, until melted and smooth. Remove from heat and whisk in eggs.

2. Stir in ground almonds and flour until blended. Stir in slivered almonds, dates and figs until evenly distributed. Pour into prepared baking pan.

3. Bake in preheated oven for 45 minutes or until a tester inserted in the center comes out with a few moist crumbs clinging to it. Let cool completely in pan on a wire rack. Remove from pan and cut into squares.

Cakes

Magic Mud Cake

The preparation time for this cake is very short, and its light and airy consistency will delight your guests! Serve warm or cold, with plain yogurt or low-fat ricotta cheese.

Tip
You can replace the whole wheat flour with ground almonds.

- *Preheat oven to 350°F (180°C)*
- *6-cup (1.5 L) baking dish*

¾ cup	unsweetened cocoa powder, divided	175 mL
¼ cup	all-purpose flour	50 mL
¼ cup	whole wheat flour	50 mL
¾ tsp	baking powder	3 mL
½ tsp	ground cinnamon	2 mL
¼ tsp	salt	1 mL
¼ cup	light butter	50 mL
½ cup	xylitol, divided	125 mL
2 cups	soy milk or skim milk, divided	500 mL

1. In a bowl, combine half the cocoa and the all-purpose flour, whole wheat flour, baking powder, cinnamon and salt.

2. In a small saucepan, combine butter, half the xylitol and half the milk. Melt over low heat, stirring occasionally. Pour over the flour mixture and stir until blended. Pour batter into baking dish and carefully drizzle the remaining milk over top.

3. In a bowl, combine the remaining cocoa and xylitol and sprinkle over the milk.

4. Bake in preheated oven for 45 to 50 minutes or until a tester inserted in the center comes out clean.

Chocolate Cake That Children Adore

Serves 4 to 6

While there are countless recipes for chocolate cake, this one is very simple and incredibly good. Let your children help you prepare it!

- *Preheat oven to 350°F (180°C)*
- *9-inch (23 cm) round cake pan, buttered*

7 oz	high-quality bittersweet (dark) chocolate	200 g
⅓ cup	butter	75 mL
¾ cup	xylitol	175 mL
1 tbsp	all-purpose flour	15 mL
5	eggs, separated	5
Pinch	salt	Pinch

1. In a microwave-safe bowl, combine chocolate and butter. Microwave on Medium-Low (30%) power, stirring every 30 seconds, until melted (or melt in the top of a double boiler over simmering water). Set aside.

2. In a large bowl, combine xylitol and flour. Whisk in egg yolks, then stir in the chocolate mixture.

3. In another bowl, using an electric mixer, beat egg whites and salt until stiff peaks form. Fold one-quarter of the egg whites into the batter, then fold in the remaining whites just until blended. Spread into prepared pan, smoothing top.

4. Bake in preheated oven for 20 minutes or until a tester inserted in the center comes out with a few moist crumbs clinging to it. Let cool in pan on a wire rack for 10 minutes. Turn out onto rack. Serve warm or let cool completely.

Pear and Fig Chocolate Cake

Who doesn't like chocolate cake with pears? To make a lighter version, we use soy milk, brown rice flour instead of wheat flour, and unsweetened cocoa mixed with dried figs instead of chocolate.

Tip

If you want the cake to be sweeter, you can add 1 tbsp (15 mL) liquid honey or 2 tsp (10 mL) agave syrup to the cocoa mixture.

- *Preheat oven to 350°F (180°C)*
- *9-inch (23 cm) round cake pan, buttered and dusted with flour*

2	large sweet pears	2
	Juice of 1 lemon	
⅓ cup	dried figs	75 mL
¾ cup	unsweetened cocoa powder	175 mL
½ cup	butter, softened, divided	125 mL
2	eggs, separated	2
1 cup	brown rice flour	250 mL
1 tbsp	baking powder	15 mL
7 tbsp	soy milk	105 mL

1. Thinly slice pears and sprinkle with lemon juice to prevent them from turning brown. Set aside.

2. In a bowl, cover figs with warm water and let soak for 15 minutes. Drain and purée in a blender. Set aside.

3. In a small saucepan, combine cocoa, ½ cup (125 mL) water and 1 tbsp (15 mL) of the butter. Heat over low heat until smooth. Stir in fig purée and cook, stirring, for 2 minutes. Let cool.

4. In a bowl, whisk together the remaining butter and egg yolks. Pour in the cocoa mixture and beat until well blended. Stir in rice flour and baking powder. Gradually add milk, stirring constantly.

5. In another bowl, using an electric mixer, beat egg whites until stiff peaks form. Fold one-quarter of the egg whites into the batter, then fold in the remaining whites just until blended.

6. Drain the juice from pears. Pour half the batter into the prepared pan, then cover with the pears. Pour the remaining batter over pears and smooth top.

7. Bake in preheated oven for 40 minutes or until a tester inserted in the center comes out clean. Let cool completely in pan on a wire rack.

Angel Cake
with Chocolate Coulis

Coulis is a French name for fruit or chocolate sauce. It comes from the Italian colare (to strain).

Tip
The mold must be perfectly clean (and definitely not greased) to allow the cake to rise properly.

Variation
For a lighter version, instead of the chocolate coulis, sprinkle strawberries or raspberries over the cake.

- *Preheat oven to 350°F (180°C)*
- *5- to 6-cup (1.25 to 1.5 L) savarin mold*

½ cup	all-purpose flour	125 mL
1 cup	xylitol, divided	250 mL
5	egg whites, at room temperature	5
Pinch	salt	Pinch

Chocolate Coulis

3½ oz	unsweetened chocolate, chopped	105 g
6 tbsp	heavy or whipping (35%) cream	90 mL
¼ cup	xylitol	50 mL
	OR	
3 tbsp	agave syrup	45 mL
2 tbsp	butter, cut into small pieces	25 mL

1. In a bowl, sift together flour and half the xylitol; set aside.

2. In a large bowl, using an electric mixer, beat egg whites and salt until soft peaks form. Gradually add the remaining xylitol, a little bit at a time, beating until stiff peaks form. Fold in the flour mixture in two additions. Pour into mold and smooth top.

3. Bake in preheated oven for 30 minutes or until a tester inserted in the center comes out clean. Carefully slide a spatula along the edges of the cake to loosen it from the mold and turn the cake out onto a wire rack to cool.

4. *Prepare the coulis:* In a saucepan, melt chocolate, cream, the natural sugar of your choice and butter over low heat, stirring constantly, until smooth.

5. Transfer cake to a serving plate and pour coulis over top. Serve immediately.

Florentines with Coconut

*Florentines were
created at the court
of Versailles under
Louis XIV during a visit
made by the Medici
(who came from
Florence).*

Variation
You can replace the
peanuts with toasted
pecans, almonds or any
other kind of nut.

- *Preheat oven to 350°F (180°C)*
- *Baking sheets, lined with parchment paper*

1 cup	raisins	250 mL
2/3 cup	chopped unsalted roasted peanuts	150 mL
2/3 cup	xylitol	150 mL
1/2 cup	corn flakes cereal	125 mL
2/3 cup	coconut milk	150 mL
5 oz	unsweetened chocolate, chopped	150 g
2 tbsp	agave syrup	25 mL
2/3 cup	unsweetened desiccated or shredded coconut	150 mL

1. In a bowl, combine raisins, peanuts, xylitol, corn flakes and coconut milk.

2. Drop spoonfuls at least 2 inches (5 cm) apart on prepared baking sheets.

3. Bake in preheated oven for 10 minutes or until golden. Gently remove from sheets with a spatula and transfer to a wire rack to cool.

4. In the top of a double boiler, over hot but not boiling water, melt chocolate, stirring until smooth. Stir in agave syrup.

5. Spread chocolate mixture on the bottom of each Florentine and gently press a pattern into the chocolate with a fork. Sprinkle with coconut. Place chocolate side up on a baking sheet and let the chocolate set.

Coconut Cake

Serves 6

An Indian legend claims that the coconut tree grants all your wishes. We don't know if it's true, but we still recommend this recipe, which we have adapted for light meals. This cake is a great favorite of ours and we don't hesitate to serve it for very special occasions.

Tips

We sprinkle this cake with a little more coconut a few minutes before it finishes baking. In winter, we serve it with hot or cold compote; in summer, with ice cream or a sorbet.

If stevia is available as a sweetener in your area, you can use it in this recipe by combining a pinch of stevia extract powder (or the equivalent of 1 tbsp/15 mL sugar) with the butter.

- *Preheat oven to 350°F (180°C)*
- *9-inch (23 cm) round cake pan, buttered and floured*

¾ cup	raisins	175 mL
2 cups	unsweetened desiccated coconut	500 mL
¾ cup + 1 tbsp	sifted all-purpose flour	190 mL
1 tsp	baking powder	5 mL
7 tbsp	butter, softened	105 mL
2	eggs, separated	2
2 tbsp	xylitol	25 mL
	OR	
4 tsp	agave syrup	20 mL
½ cup	finely chopped pitted dates	125 mL
3 tbsp	milk	45 mL

1. In a bowl, cover raisins with warm water and let soak for 15 minutes. Drain and finely chop.

2. In another bowl, combine coconut, flour and baking powder; set aside.

3. In a large bowl, using an electric mixer, cream butter until fluffy. Beat in egg yolks and the natural sugar of your choice until frothy. Fold in raisins and dates. Stir in milk, then the flour mixture.

4. In another bowl, using an electric mixer with clean beaters, beat egg whites until stiff peaks form. Gently fold into the batter. Pour into prepared pan and smooth top.

5. Bake in preheated oven for 75 minutes. Let cool completely in pan on a wire rack.

Light Carrot Cake with Nuts, Raisins and Cinnamon

Serves 6

The use of carrots in cakes dates to the Middle Ages. Carrot cake become popular in Great Britain during the Second World War due to rationing. Carrot cakes are best eaten the day they are made.

Tip

If stevia is available as a sweetener in your area, you can use it in this recipe by dissolving a pinch of stevia extract powder (or the equivalent of 1 tbsp/15 mL sugar) in 1 tbsp (15 mL) water and combining it with the eggs.

Variation

You can also add dried diced figs and prunes to the batter. This will increase the sweet taste of the cake, but also its calorie content!

- *Preheat oven to 350°F (180°C)*
- *9-inch (23 cm) round cake pan, buttered*

1 cup + 2 tbsp	sifted all-purpose flour	275 mL
1 tbsp	baking powder	15 mL
1 tsp	ground cinnamon	5 mL
3	eggs	3
1 tbsp	liquid honey or xylitol OR	15 mL
2 tsp	agave syrup	10 mL
7 tbsp	light butter, melted	105 mL
4	carrots, grated	4
¾ cup	chopped nuts	175 mL
½ cup	sultana raisins	125 mL

1. In a bowl, combine flour, baking powder and cinnamon.

2. In a large bowl, using an electric mixer, beat eggs and the natural sugar of your choice until frothy. Stir in flour mixture. Stir in butter until smooth. Stir in carrots, nuts and raisins. Pour into prepared pan and smooth top.

3. Bake in preheated oven for 40 minutes or until a tester inserted in the center comes out clean. Let cool in pan on a wire rack for 15 minutes. Turn out onto rack to cool completely.

Carrot and Hazelnut Cake with Cheese Garnish

Serves 4		

We prepare this carrot cake, our favorite, with soy or corn flour mixed with ground hazelnuts. It is delicious as an afternoon snack, with a cup of mint tea.

Tip

If stevia is available as a sweetener in your area, you can use it in this recipe by dissolving ⅛ tsp (0.5 mL) stevia extract powder (or the equivalent of 2 tbsp/ 25 mL sugar) in 2 tbsp (25 mL) soy milk or milk and adding it to the butter.

Variation

You can replace the chopped hazelnuts with chopped almonds and the ground hazelnuts with ground almonds.

- *Preheat oven to 350°F (180°C)*
- *6-inch (15 cm) round cake pan, buttered and bottom lined with parchment paper*

¼ cup	light butter, softened or hazelnut oil	50 mL
2 tbsp	xylitol	25 mL
	OR	
4 tsp	agave syrup	20 mL
½ cup	ground hazelnuts	125 mL
¼ cup	soy flour or corn flour, sifted	50 mL
1½ tsp	baking powder	7 mL
1	carrot, finely grated	1
⅓ cup	chopped hazelnuts	75 mL
2	eggs	2

Garnish

¾ cup	light smooth ricotta cheese	175 mL
1 tbsp	liquid honey	15 mL
	OR	
2 tsp	agave syrup	10 mL

1. In a bowl, using a wooden spoon, cream butter and the natural sugar of your choice. Stir in ground hazelnuts, soy flour and baking powder until blended. Stir in carrot and chopped hazelnuts. Stir in eggs, one at a time. Pour into prepared pan and smooth top.

2. Bake in preheated oven for 35 minutes. Cover with parchment paper and bake for 20 minutes or until a tester inserted in the center comes out clean. Let cool in pan on a wire rack for 15 minutes. Turn out onto rack to cool completely.

3. *Prepare the garnish:* In a bowl, combine ricotta and the natural sugar of your choice. Spread over cake. Refrigerate for about 1 hour, until chilled, or for up to 8 hours.

Carrot Cake with Mascarpone

Serves 6

We discovered this
cake in New York and
immediately loved it.
Every evening, the
journey back to the
hotel led us past a
small mini-market run
by German immigrants.
It was a true Ali Baba
cave of wonders for
us, tired from traipsing
for hours through the
city! It was filled with
delicious specialties.
Among them was
this wonderful
cake, topped with
mascarpone and nuts.
We adapted it to make
it lighter.

Tip
Keep this cake in the
refrigerator until you're
ready to serve it.

Variation
For an even lighter
version, use low-fat
whipped cream instead
of mascarpone.

- *Preheat oven to 350°F (180°C)*
- *9-inch (23 cm) round cake pan, buttered and lined with parchment paper*

¾ cup	whole wheat flour	175 mL
¾ cup	cake flour	175 mL
1 tbsp	baking powder	15 mL
½ tsp	salt	2 mL
2	eggs, beaten	2
2	bananas, puréed	2
¾ cup	hazelnut oil	175 mL
4	carrots, grated	4
½ cup	chopped walnuts	125 mL
⅓ cup	raisins	75 mL

Topping

1 cup	mascarpone cheese	250 mL
¼ cup	chopped walnuts	50 mL
2 tbsp	liquid honey	25 mL

1. In a bowl, combine whole wheat flour, cake flour, baking powder and salt.

2. In another bowl, using an electric mixer, beat eggs, bananas and hazelnut oil until well combined. Stir in flour mixture. Stir in carrots, walnuts and raisins. Pour into prepared pan and smooth top.

3. Bake in preheated oven for 60 minutes or until a tester inserted in the center comes out clean. Let cool in pan on a wire rack for 15 minutes. Turn out onto rack to cool completely.

4. *Prepare the topping:* In a bowl, combine mascarpone, walnuts and honey. Spread over top and sides of the cake.

Summer Cheesecake

	Serves 6	

The history of cheesecake takes us back to Ancient Greece. The first mention of it appears in De Agri Cultura *by Roman statesman Marcus Porcius Cato, who is said to have discovered cheesecake at the Olympic Games in Greece.*

Tip

The cake may sink in the center while it's baking, but that's normal. Fill the indentation with cream and fruit.

- *Preheat oven to 325°F (160°C)*
- *9-inch (23 cm) springform pan, buttered*

8	bran or oat crackers, crumbled (about 1 cup/250 mL)	8
4	eggs, separated	4
⅓ cup	sifted all-purpose flour	75 mL
1 lb	light ricotta cheese	500 g
2 tbsp	liquid honey	25 mL
2 cups	milk (approx.)	500 mL
	Grated zest of 1 orange	
	Unsweetened whipped cream	
	Fresh fruit	

1. Press cracker crumbs into bottom of prepared pan.

2. In a bowl, combine egg yolks, flour, ricotta and honey. Gradually stir in enough milk to make a smooth batter (the quantity will depend on the consistency of the cheese). Stir in orange zest.

3. In another bowl, using an electric mixer, beat egg whites until stiff peaks form. Fold one-quarter of the egg whites into the batter, then fold in the remaining whites just until blended. Pour over cracker crumbs and smooth top.

4. Bake in preheated oven for 60 to 75 minutes or until set. Turn off the oven and let cool in the oven for 1 hour. Remove from oven and let cool completely in pan on a wire rack.

5. Just before serving, decorate the top with whipped cream and a selection of soft fruits.

Lemon Cheesecake

● ●

Serves 8

This recipe is very light and absolutely delicious. Our friends love it!

Tips

For the crust, you can use cookies from one of our recipes (see pages 86–90).

If stevia is available as a sweetener in your area, you can use it in the crust by adding a pinch of stevia extract powder (or the equivalent of 2 tsp/10 mL sugar) with the butter. For the filling, add ¼ tsp (1 mL) stevia extract powder (or the equivalent of ⅓ cup/ 75 mL sugar) with the eggs and add ⅓ cup (75 mL) extra yogurt.

- *Preheat oven to 300°F (150°C)*
- *9-inch (23 cm) tart pan with removable bottom, lined with parchment paper*

Crust

2 tbsp	butter	25 mL
2 tsp	xylitol	10 mL
	OR	
1½ tsp	agave syrup	7 mL
½ cup	ground almonds	125 mL
¼ cup	crumbled oatmeal or bran cookies	50 mL
¼ cup	chopped hazelnuts	50 mL
2 tsp	ground cinnamon	10 mL

Filling

4	medium eggs	4
⅓ cup	xylitol	75 mL
	OR	
¼ cup	agave syrup	50 mL
¼ cup	cornstarch	15 mL
2 cups	low-fat fromage frais (unripened fresh cheese)	500 mL
½ cup	plain yogurt	125 mL
	Grated zest of 1 lemon	
	Juice of 2 lemons	

1. *Prepare the crust:* In a saucepan, heat butter and the natural sugar of your choice over low heat, stirring until melted. Remove from heat and stir in almonds, cookie crumbs, hazelnuts and cinnamon until well combined. Press evenly into bottom and sides of prepared pan, pressing down firmly.

2. Bake in preheated oven for 10 minutes or until golden. Let cool in pan on a wire rack. Increase the oven temperature to 325°F (160°C).

3. *Prepare the filling:* In a bowl, using an electric mixer, beat eggs and the natural sugar of your choice. Beat in cornstarch, cheese, yogurt, lemon zest and lemon juice until creamy. Pour into crust and smooth top.

4. Bake for 40 to 45 minutes or until set. Let cool completely in pan on a wire rack.

Chocolate Raisin Cheesecake

Serves 8

This is our favorite cheesecake, and it is always a great success. We use ricotta cheese for the filling, and a mixture of flour and cornmeal for the crust.

Variations

You can use ground oats instead of cornmeal to prepare the crust.

Using agave syrup rather than maple syrup will make a lighter cake.

For a lighter version, replace the icing with a raspberry or blackberry sauce and decorate with summer fruits.

- *Preheat oven to 325°F (160°C)*
- *9-inch (23 cm) tart pan with removable bottom, buttered*

Crust

½ cup	all-purpose flour	125 mL
⅓ cup	very fine cornmeal	75 mL
2 tbsp	unsweetened cocoa powder	25 mL
½ cup	light butter, softened	125 mL
⅓ cup	finely chopped pitted dates	75 mL

Filling

2	eggs, beaten	2
1 cup	ricotta cheese	250 mL
½ cup	plain yogurt	125 mL
2 tbsp	pure maple syrup	25 mL
	OR	
4 tsp	agave syrup	20 mL
½ cup	raisins	125 mL

Icing

½ cup	unsweetened cocoa powder	125 mL
3 tbsp	butter, melted	45 mL
2 tbsp	pure maple syrup	25 mL
	OR	
4 tsp	agave syrup	20 mL

1. *Prepare the crust:* In a bowl, combine flour, cornmeal and cocoa. Add butter and dates and work with your fingers to obtain a dough of even consistency.

2. On a floured work surface, roll out the dough and fit into prepared pan. Prick the base and sides with a fork. Bake in preheated oven for 15 minutes or until firm.

3. *Prepare the filling:* In a large bowl, whisk together eggs, cheese, yogurt and the natural sugar of your choice. Stir in raisins. Spread over crust. Bake for 30 to 35 minutes or until the top is lightly browned.

4. *Prepare the icing:* In a saucepan, combine cocoa, butter and the natural sugar of your choice. Melt over low heat, stirring until smooth. Pour over the hot filling and smooth the surface. Let cool completely in pan on a wire rack.

Roma Cheesecake

In Rome, just next to the Pantheon, there is a cake shop that serves this delicious ricotta cake. Ricotta is made with the whey created in the production of other cheeses. The whey is cooked again to obtain this light cheese, hence its name (in Italian, ricotta means "recooked"). Our version of this cake is lighter than the traditional Roman cheesecake.

Tips

Make bread crumbs with toasted day-old whole wheat bread. Let cool and grind to find crumbs in a food processor.

This cake, drizzled with a strawberry or raspberry sauce, makes a great light snack.

If stevia is available as a sweetener in your area, you can use it in this recipe by dissolving ⅛ tsp (0.5 mL) stevia extract powder (or the equivalent of 2 tbsp/ 25 mL sugar) in 2 tbsp (25 mL) water or orange juice and adding it to the ricotta mixture.

- Preheat oven to 375°F (190°C)
- 8-inch (20 cm) tart pan with removable bottom, buttered

1 tbsp	fine dry bread crumbs (see tip, at left)	15 ml
1 tbsp	raisins	15 mL
2	eggs, separated	2
1¼ cups	ricotta or other soft cream cheese	300 mL
2 tbsp	finely chopped dried apricots or prunes	25 mL
2 tbsp	xylitol or liquid honey OR	25 mL
4 tsp	agave syrup	20 mL
	Grated zest of 1 orange	

1. Sprinkle prepared pan with bread crumbs, covering the base and sides. Set aside.
2. In a bowl, cover raisins with hot water and let soak for 15 minutes to soften. Drain well.
3. In another bowl, combine egg yolks and ricotta. Stir in raisins, apricots, the natural sugar of your choice and orange zest.
4. In another bowl, using an electric mixer, beat egg whites until stiff peaks form. Gently fold into the batter. Pour into prepared pan and smooth top.
5. Bake in preheated oven for 1 hour or until puffed and set. Remove tart ring from pan and let cake cool completely on base on a wire rack.

Light Ricotta Cake

Serves 6

This cake is gluten-free, since we use brown rice flour, which you can find in most health food stores.

Tip

We don't add the honey to this cake because the spices give it plenty of taste and the bananas are naturally sweet, but you can add it if you prefer.

- *Preheat oven to 350°F (180°C)*
- *8-inch (20 cm) round cake pan, lined with parchment paper*

3	eggs, separated	3
3	bananas, puréed	3
1 lb	light ricotta cheese	500 g
1 tbsp	liquid honey (optional)	15 mL
	Grated zest of 1 lemon	
1/4 cup	brown rice flour	50 mL
1 tsp	baking powder	5 mL
1/4 tsp	mixed spices (ground cinnamon, cardamom and ginger)	1 mL
Pinch	salt	Pinch

1. In a large bowl, whisk egg yolks until pale. Whisk in bananas, ricotta, honey (if using) and lemon zest. Stir in rice flour, baking powder and spices until evenly blended.

2. In another bowl, using an electric mixer, beat egg whites and salt until stiff peaks form. Fold one-quarter of the whites into the batter, then fold in the remaining whites just until blended. Pour into prepared pan and smooth top.

3. Bake in preheated oven for 20 minutes or until the top is golden. Let cool completely in pan on a wire rack.

Small Ricotta Cakes

*We discovered these
delicious cakes of
Italian origin in New
York's Little Italy.*

Tip
Make sure to drain the
cheese well before use.

• **Baking sheet, lined with parchment paper and lightly
floured**

Dough

1 cup	milk	250 mL
1	vanilla bean, split	1
1/4 tsp	salt	1 mL
4 cups	sifted all-purpose flour	1 L
1 1/4 oz	brewer's yeast	35 g
1/2 cup	warm water	125 mL
2	eggs, beaten	2
7 tbsp	butter, melted	105 mL
2 tbsp	liquid honey	25 mL

Filling

1 tbsp	raisins	15 mL
2	egg yolks	2
14 oz	ricotta or fresh goat cheese, drained	400 g
	Grated zest of 1 lemon	

1. *Prepare the dough:* In a saucepan, heat milk, vanilla
   bean and salt over low heat until warm to the
   touch. Discard vanilla bean.

2. In a bowl, combine yeast and warm water.

3. Place flour in a large bowl and make a well in the
   center. Gently pour in the yeast mixture, then the
   warmed milk, stirring gently until combined. Add
   eggs, butter and honey and work with your fingers
   until dough is smooth and comes loose from the
   edges of the bowl. Cover with a damp cloth and let
   rise in a warm place for 1 1/2 hours.

4. *Prepare the filling:* Meanwhile, in a small bowl,
   cover raisins with warm water and let soak for
   15 minutes. Drain well.

5. In another bowl, combine egg yolks, ricotta, lemon
   zest and raisins; set aside.

Tip

When rolling the dough, if it's too springy, let it rest for a few minutes to relax.

6. On a lightly floured work surface, roll out dough and divide into 20 small rounds. Place at least 1 inch (2.5 cm) apart on prepared baking sheet. Let rise for 15 to 20 minutes. Meanwhile, preheat oven to 400°F (200°C).

7. Make a small hollow in the center of each round and fill each with 2 tsp (10 mL) filling.

8. Bake for about 20 minutes or until puffed and golden brown.

Paddy Cake with Polenta, Raisins, Ricotta and Dates

• •

Serves 8

Polenta made from cornmeal is a typical Northern Italian dish. In Corsica, polenta is made with chestnut flour.

Tips
We prefer to remove the dry skin from the outside of the dates before chopping them, but this is not required.

This cake keeps for 3 days at room temperature, well-wrapped and protected from the air.

Variation
Prunes can replace the dates.

• Preheat oven to 340°F (170°C)
• 9-inch (23 cm) round cake pan, buttered and floured

¼ cup	raisins	50 mL
2 cups	all-purpose flour	500 mL
½ cup	cornmeal (polenta)	125 mL
4 tsp	baking powder	20 mL
1 tsp	salt	5 mL
2	eggs, separated, yolks whisked	2
1 cup	ricotta cheese	250 mL
½ cup	butter, softened, cut into small pieces	125 mL
1 cup	chopped pitted dates	250 mL

1. In a bowl, cover raisins with warm water and let soak for 15 minutes. Drain and set aside.

2. In a large bowl, combine flour, cornmeal, baking powder and salt. Stir in egg yolks and ricotta. Add butter and 1 cup (250 mL) water. Using an electric mixer, beat until batter is smooth.

3. In a separate bowl, using an electric mixer with clean beaters, beat egg whites until stiff peaks form. Fold one-quarter of the egg whites into the batter, then carefully fold in the remaining egg whites just until blended. Fold in raisins and dates. Pour into prepared pan and smooth top.

4. Bake in preheated oven for 45 minutes. Cover with parchment paper and bake for about 1 hour or until a tester inserted in the center comes out clean. Let cool in pan on a wire rack for 15 minutes. Turn out onto rack to cool completely.

Yogurt and Ricotta Cake

Serve this light and delicious cake for breakfast (as they do in Italy) or for afternoon tea.

Tip
Use fat-free plain, unsweetened yogurt for this recipe.

- *Preheat oven to 400°F (200°C)*
- *8-inch (20 cm) square cake pan, buttered*

3	eggs	3
1/2 cup	plain yogurt	125 mL
1/2 cup	cornstarch	125 mL
6 tbsp	agave syrup	90 mL
1 1/2 cups	dry pressed ricotta cheese, crumbled	375 mL

1. Separate 2 of the eggs and set the yolks and whites aside separately. Beat the third egg in a separate bowl.

2. Place yogurt in a saucepan and sift cornstarch over top; whisk until blended. Whisk in agave syrup. Cook over low heat, stirring constantly, for about 5 minutes or until thickened. Stir in ricotta. Transfer to a large bowl and let cool.

3. In a bowl, using an electric mixer, beat egg whites until stiff peaks form.

4. Whisk egg yolks into the ricotta mixture, then fold in egg whites. Pour into prepared pan and smooth top. Brush with beaten egg.

5. Bake in preheated oven for 30 minutes or until puffed and golden and a tester inserted in the center comes out clean. Let cool completely in pan on a wire rack.

Mascarpone Fruitcake

Cakes iced with maple syrup are a Canadian inspiration. Maple syrup is, however, rich in carbohydrates, so if that's a concern for you, replace it with agave syrup, which has a very low glycemic index.

Tips

When serving, you can decorate the top of the cake with seasonal fruits, such as raspberries, blueberries or wild strawberries.

In the icing, you can use 2 tbsp (25 mL) agave syrup instead of the maple syrup.

- *Preheat oven to 350°F (180°C)*
- *9-inch (23 cm) springform pan, bottom lined with parchment paper*

½ cup	chopped pitted dates	125 mL
½ cup	sultana raisins	125 mL
1 cup	hot green tea	250 mL
4	eggs	4
2⅓ cups	whole wheat flour	575 mL
1 cup	light butter, softened and cut into small pieces	250 mL
1½ tbsp	baking powder	22 mL
1 tsp	salt	5 mL
½ tsp	ground ginger	2 mL
	Grated zest of 1 orange	

Icing

2 cups	light ricotta cheese	500 mL
3 tbsp	mascarpone cheese	45 mL
3 tbsp	maple syrup	45 mL

1. In a bowl, soak dates and raisins in green tea for 15 minutes. Drain and set aside.

2. In a large bowl, using an electric mixer, beat eggs, flour, butter, baking powder, salt, ginger and orange zest until well blended. Stir in dates and raisins. Spread in prepared pan, smoothing top.

3. Bake in preheated oven for 60 to 75 minutes or until cake has risen and the top springs back when lightly touched. Let cool in pan on a wire rack for 15 minutes. Turn out onto rack, peel off parchment paper and let cool completely.

4. *Prepare the icing:* In a bowl, whisk together ricotta, mascarpone and maple syrup.

5. Cut the cake horizontally into two or three layers, depending on its height. Spread each layer and the top with icing. Refrigerate until you're ready to serve, up to 8 hours.

Dried Fruit Cake

This recipe is a variation
of the traditional
dried fruit cake ring
found in Italian cake
shops, especially in the
province of Umbria. It
is excellent as a snack,
with raspberry sauce
and ricotta cheese or
yogurt.

Tip
Because of the
sweetness of the dried
fruit, there's no need
to add sugar to this
fruitcake, but if you want
it to be sweeter, add the
optional agave syrup or
1 tbsp (15 mL) liquid
honey.

- Preheat oven to 410°F (210°C)
- 8-inch (20 cm) round cake pan, buttered and dusted with flour

4	eggs, separated	4
1 cup	butter, softened	250 mL
2 tsp	agave syrup (optional)	10 mL
1½ cups	all-purpose flour	375 mL
1 tbsp	ground cinnamon	15 mL
½ cup	finely chopped pitted dates	125 mL
⅓ cup	finely chopped dried figs	75 mL
⅓ cup	finely chopped dried apricots	75 mL
¼ cup	raisins	50 mL
	Grated zest of 1 lemon	

1. In a bowl, using an electric mixer, beat egg yolks, butter and agave syrup (if using) until well blended. Stir in flour and cinnamon. Stir in dates, figs, apricots, raisins and lemon zest.

2. In another bowl, using an electric mixer with clean beaters, beat egg whites until stiff peaks form. Fold one-quarter of the egg whites into the batter, then carefully fold in the remaining whites just until blended. Pour into the prepared pan and smooth top.

3. Bake in preheated oven for 30 minutes or until a tester inserted in the center comes out clean. Let cool in pan on a wire rack for 15 minutes. Turn out onto rack to cool completely.

Tasty Tiny Fruitcakes

The word "cake" has a Viking origin — it comes from Norse kaka.

Tip
You can use frozen fruit; just omit the lemon juice.

Variation
If you prefer, you can make one large cake in a 6-cup (1.5 L) baking dish. Increase the baking time to about 40 minutes.

- *Preheat oven to 350°F (180°C)*
- *Six ³/₄-cup (175 mL) ramekins, buttered*

Filling

8	small plums, halved	8
3	apples, peeled and diced	3
1 cup	blueberries	250 mL
¹/₃ cup	xylitol	75 mL
	OR	
¹/₄ cup	agave syrup	50 mL
2 tbsp	freshly squeezed lemon juice	25 mL

Topping

1	egg	1
1¹/₄ cups	all-purpose flour	300 mL
1¹/₂ tsp	baking powder	7 mL
¹/₂ tsp	salt	2 mL
¹/₃ cup	xylitol	75 mL
	OR	
¹/₄ cup	agave syrup	50 mL
¹/₃ cup	melted butter	75 mL
¹/₄ cup	milk	50 mL
¹/₄ cup	water	50 mL

1. *Prepare the filling:* In a large bowl, combine plums, apples, blueberries, the natural sugar of your choice and lemon juice. Spoon evenly into prepared ramekins. Place ramekins on a baking sheet.

2. *Prepare the topping:* In a bowl, whisk together egg, flour, baking powder, salt, the natural sugar of your choice, butter, milk and water. Pour evenly over the filling.

3. Bake in preheated oven for 20 to 25 minutes or until a tester inserted in the center of a ramekin comes out clean. Serve warm or cold.

Pear Flan

For the evening meal, we often prepare this small, economical dessert, which can be made very quickly and which we eat with a few small corn flake or oat flake cookies.

Variation
You can substitute apples for the pears.

- *Preheat oven to 350°F (180°C)*
- *8-inch (20 cm) glass or ceramic quiche dish, buttered*

2	eggs	2
2 cups	milk	500 mL
3 tbsp	whole wheat flour	45 mL
Pinch	ground cardamom	Pinch
Pinch	ground cinnamon	Pinch
3	small sweet pears, peeled and diced	3

1. In a bowl, using an electric mixer, beat eggs until foamy. Beat in milk. Beat in flour, cardamom and cinnamon. Stir in pears. Pour into prepared dish.

2. Bake in preheated oven for about 40 minutes or until puffed and golden and a tester inserted in the center comes out clean. Serve warm or cool.

Prune Flan

This flan, with a filling of ground almonds and crème fraîche, is very elegant, despite its apparent simplicity.

Tips

If you can, buy prunes with the pit still in; pitted prunes are chemically treated.

Choose sweet oranges to add depth of taste to this cake.

If the filling is not sweet enough for your taste, add 2 tsp (10 mL) xylitol or 1 tsp (5 mL) stevia or agave syrup.

- *Preheat oven to 400°F (200°C)*
- *8-inch (20 cm) tart pan with removable bottom, buttered*

1 ½ cups	prunes	375 mL
	Juice of 2 oranges	
9 oz	Pâte Brisée (see recipe, page 16)	270 g
2	eggs	2
¾ cup	ground almonds	175 mL
⅔ cup	crème fraîche	150 mL

1. In a bowl, combine prunes and orange juice. Let soak for 30 minutes or until softened. Drain, reserving juice.

2. Meanwhile, on a lightly floured work surface, roll out pastry and fit into prepared pan. Prick the bottom with a fork. Bake in preheated oven for 12 minutes or until golden and firm. Let cool slightly. Reduce oven temperature to 350°F (180°C).

3. In a bowl, whisk eggs until blended. Whisk in almonds, crème fraîche and reserved juice.

4. Arrange prunes in tart shell and pour the almond mixture over top. Bake for 30 minutes or until filling is set. Let cool slightly in pan on a wire rack. Serve warm.

Summer Cherry Charlotte

Serves 4

This cake is said to have been created for Queen Charlotte, the wife of King George III of England.

Tip
Add the agave syrup if you don't find the cherries sweet enough.

• *6-cup (1.5 L) charlotte mold*

1¼ lbs	sweet cherries, pitted	625 g
6 tbsp	unsweetened apple juice	90 mL
2 tsp	agave syrup (optional)	10 mL
3 tbsp	butter	45 mL
2 tbsp	sesame oil	25 mL
11	thick slices whole wheat bread, crusts removed	11
	Ricotta cheese or plain yogurt	

1. In a bowl, toss cherries with apple juice and agave syrup (if using). Let stand for 30 minutes. Meanwhile, preheat oven to 375°F (190°C).

2. In a small saucepan, melt butter over low heat. Remove from heat and stir in sesame oil. Brush the charlotte mold with a thin layer of this mixture.

3. Brush one side of 6 slices of bread with the butter mixture and line the bottom and sides of the mold, with the buttered side facing the mold. Spoon in cherries and sprinkle with the collected juice.

4. Cut a large circle out of one slice of bread and place it on top of the cherries. Cut the remaining slices into smaller rounds and arrange them around the large circle to cover completely. Brush with butter mixture.

5. Bake for 35 to 40 minutes or until the top is golden and crusty. Serve hot or warm with ricotta or yogurt.

Peach and Raspberry Financiers

A classic French pastry, the financier is a rich almond cake that is traditionally baked in the shape of a gold bar. Here, we have added fruit to make it lighter and more savory.

Variation
Use any seasonal fresh fruits or even soaked dried fruits.

- *Preheat oven to 460°F (240°C)*
- *Four 1-cup (250 mL) ramekins or other small baking dishes*

1 cup	xylitol	250 mL
½ cup	all-purpose flour	125 mL
½ cup	ground almonds	125 mL
4	egg whites	4
½ cup	butter, melted	125 mL
2	peaches	2
2 cups	raspberries	500 mL

1. In a bowl, combine xylitol, flour and ground almonds. Using an electric mixer, vigorously beat in egg whites. Beat in butter. Gently stir in peaches and raspberries. Pour into ramekins.

2. Bake in preheated oven for 10 minutes. Reduce oven temperature to 410°F (210°C) and bake for 10 minutes. Turn off the heat and leave the financiers in the oven for 5 minutes. Serve warm.

Corn Cake with Syrup

Our friend Micheline, who breeds magnificent Maine Coon cats in her charming home near Bourges, gave us this low-calorie recipe designed for people with wheat and dairy allergies.

Tip
This cake is best served warm, topped with light cream.

- *Preheat oven to 400°F (200°C)*
- *6-inch (15 cm) round cake pan, buttered*

5 tbsp	cornstarch	65 mL
1 tbsp	baking powder	15 mL
2 tbsp	soy milk	25 mL
2 tbsp	vegetable oil	25 mL
1	egg, beaten	1
2	sweet apples or firm pears, peeled and diced.	2

Glaze

1	egg	1
⅓ cup	melted butter	75 mL
3 tbsp	pure maple syrup	45 mL
	OR	
2 tbsp	agave syrup	25 mL

1. In a bowl, whisk together cornstarch, baking powder, milk and oil. Whisk in egg until batter is smooth and somewhat elastic. Pour into prepared pan and arrange apples on top in two layers.

2. *Prepare the glaze:* In a bowl, whisk together egg, butter and the natural sugar of your choice. Pour over the apples.

3. Bake in preheated oven for 20 to 30 minutes or until golden. (Don't overcook; the cake should be moist.)

Rice Cakes

We make these cakes with brown rice. The yogurt gives them protein and their creamy consistency.

Variation
You can replace the pecans with unsalted pistachios.

• *Two 1-cup (250 mL) ramekins or other heatproof dishes*

¾ cup	brown rice	175 mL
1 cup	water	250 mL
⅓ cup	plain yogurt	75 mL
⅓ cup	raisins	75 mL
¼ tsp	ground cinnamon	1 mL
⅓ cup	chopped pecans	75 mL

1. In a saucepan, bring rice and water to a boil over high heat. Reduce heat and boil gently until rice is al dente.

2. Remove from heat and stir in yogurt, raisins and cinnamon. Spread into ramekins and sprinkle with pecans. Refrigerate for at least 8 hours or for up to 1 day.

Coconut and Pecan Brownies (page 99)

Lemon Cheesecake (page 112)

Fruity Delights

Strawberries in Cherry Sauce

We love walking in the markets when the summer fruit season arrives. The bright colors and enticing flavors provide endless inspiration for new desserts.

Tip
This simple little dessert is delicious served very cold.

2 lbs	sweet cherries, pitted (about 4 1/2 cups/1.125 L)	1 kg
6 cups	strawberries, hulled	1.5 L
	Crème fraîche or unsweetened whipped cream	
1/4 cup	slivered almonds, toasted	50 mL
	Fresh mint leaves	

1. In a saucepan, combine cherries and 1/2 cup (125 mL) water. Bring to a simmer over medium heat. Cover, reduce heat to low and simmer, stirring occasionally, for about 15 minutes or until very soft. Transfer to a blender and purée until smooth. Let cool.

2. Pour cherry sauce into individual bowls and arrange strawberries on top. Decorate with crème fraîche, almonds and mint leaves.

Iced Red Berries with Hot Blueberry Sauce

This little delicacy is undoubtedly the easiest to prepare out of all our dessert recipes. It has an amusing air and is sure to delight your guests.

Tips

The berries should be in bite-size pieces, so you may need to cut them up a bit.

If your freezer is very cold, transfer the frozen berries to the refrigerator 30 minutes before serving.

It is important that the sauce is very hot so that the frozen fruit begins to melt instantly.

1 cup	blackberries	250 mL
1 cup	strawberries, hulled	250 mL
1 cup	raspberries	250 mL
1 cup	gooseberries	250 mL
3½ cups	blueberries	875 mL
	Freshly squeezed juice of 1 orange	

1. Arrange blackberries, strawberries, raspberries and gooseberries on a freezer-safe serving platter and freeze for at least 2 hours, until firm, or for up to 1 day.

2. In a small saucepan, bring blueberries and orange juice to a simmer over low heat. Simmer, stirring occasionally, for 10 to 15 minutes or until blueberries are very soft. Transfer to a blender and purée until smooth.

3. Remove the fruit from the freezer, divide among serving dishes and spoon hot blueberry sauce on top.

Iced Red Berries with Hot Chocolate Sauce

For gourmet eaters, among whom we certainly count ourselves, we've replaced the blueberry sauce with a rich chocolate sauce.

Tips

High-quality cocoa powder contributes greatly to this delicious dessert, so choose well.

If stevia is available as a sweetener in your area, you can use it in this recipe by dissolving 1/4 tsp (1 mL) stevia extract powder (or the equivalent of 3 tbsp/ 45 mL sugar) in 3 tbsp (45 mL) extra soy milk and adding it to the cocoa mixture.

1 cup	black currants	250 mL
1 cup	strawberries, hulled	250 mL
1 cup	raspberries	250 mL
1 cup	gooseberries	250 mL
1 cup	unsweetened cocoa powder	250 mL
3 tbsp	liquid honey or xylitol OR	45 mL
2 tbsp	agave syrup	25 mL
3 tbsp	soy milk	45 mL
1 tsp	light butter or mascarpone cheese	5 mL

1. Arrange currants, strawberries, raspberries and gooseberries on a freezer-safe serving platter and freeze for at least 2 hours, until firm, or for up to 1 day.

2. In the top of a double boiler, combine cocoa, 1 cup (250 mL) water, the natural sugar of your choice, soy milk and butter. Cook over low heat, stirring constantly, for 5 minutes or until smooth and hot.

3. Remove the fruit from the freezer, divide among serving dishes and spoon hot chocolate sauce on top.

Melon in Strawberry Sauce

Serves 4		
1 lb	strawberries, hulled, divided	500 g
1 tbsp	lemon juice	15 mL
1	large melon (honeydew, cantaloupe, canary or other variety)	1

This simple yet succulent dessert has many potential variations: pineapple in strawberry sauce, mango in blackberry sauce, fresh figs in blueberry sauce and so on.

Tip

Serve with a few cookies or a slice of cake.

1. In a blender or food processor, purée half the strawberries and the lemon juice until smooth.

2. Peel the melon and cut it into 12 slices, trimming out seeds. Cut the remaining strawberries in half (or into quarters if large). Divide melon slices and strawberries evenly among glass plates. Pour strawberry sauce around the strawberries and melon.

"Fruitités" Cold Fruit Plate with Yogurt Sauce

Serves 2		
1 cup	plain yogurt	250 mL
2 tbsp	freshly squeezed orange juice	25 mL
	Fresh fruits, such as pitted cherries, apricots, strawberries, raspberries, figs, pears and apples	

Here is a fun recipe to try for a snack or as a great way to start off or finish a meal, inspired by the traditional French crudités (a raw vegetable platter).

Variation

If you like, add 1 tsp (5 mL) liquid honey or agave syrup to sweeten the yogurt.

1. In a bowl, combine yogurt and orange juice. Set in the center of a large serving platter. Set aside.

2. Cut larger fruits into cubes or slices. Artfully arrange fruits on the platter around the bowl of yogurt. Refrigerate until very cold.

Fresh Fruits with Two Sauces

Serves 6

We love to serve this recipe in the summer, as it goes perfectly with a barbecue party. The sauces can be served hot, warm or at room temperature.

Tip
You can prepare this dessert the day before, keep the fruit and sauces separately in the fridge and lightly warm the sauces just before serving. Hot sauces on the cold fruit are simply delicious.

2	kiwifruit, peeled and chopped	2
2	pears, chopped	2
2	nectarines, chopped	2
2	oranges, peeled and broken into segments	2
1	small pineapple, peeled and chopped	1

Chocolate Sauce

5 oz	unsweetened chocolate, chopped	150 g
3 tbsp	agave syrup	45 mL
²⁄₃ cup	heavy or whipping (35%) cream	150 mL
½ cup	passion fruit pulp	125 mL
1	banana, mashed	1

Caramel-Ginger Sauce

²⁄₃ cup	xylitol OR	150 mL
¼ cup	agave syrup	50 mL
2 tbsp	finely chopped gingerroot	25 mL
²⁄₃ cup	heavy or whipping (35%) cream	150 mL
2 tbsp	butter	25 mL

1. In a bowl, combine kiwis, pears, nectarines, oranges and pineapple. Cover and refrigerate until ready to serve, for up to 12 hours.

2. *Prepare the chocolate sauce:* In a heatproof bowl, combine chocolate and agave syrup. In a saucepan, bring cream to a boil over medium heat; pour over the chocolate mixture and let stand for 5 minutes. Stir until smooth. Stir in passion fruit pulp and banana. Keep warm or let cool.

3. *Prepare the caramel-ginger sauce:* In a saucepan, cook the natural sugar of your choice over low heat until caramelized to an amber color. Stir in ginger, cream and butter until blended. Keep warm or let cool.

4. Divide fruit among serving bowls. Drizzle with chocolate sauce and caramel-ginger sauce.

Angels' Delight Fresh Fruit Chocolate Fondue

This dessert came from my Aunt Ella, who loved experimenting and inventing new dishes. One Sunday afternoon, we concocted this dessert, which was so simple but oh-so-delicious that we immediately dubbed it "Angels' Delight." As my aunt said, "Even the angels would have eaten it." And for my adorable Aunt Ella, that says everything.

Tip

If stevia is available as a sweetener in your area, you can use it in this recipe by dissolving a pinch of stevia extract powder (or the equivalent of 1 tbsp/15 mL sugar) in 1 tbsp (15 mL) extra soy milk or milk and adding it to the cocoa mixture.

Variation

For a lighter alternative, you can replace the chocolate sauce with strawberry sauce or, even more simply, with plain yogurt.

Sauce

1/4 cup	unsweetened cocoa powder	50 mL
6 to 8 tbsp	soy milk or skim milk	90 to 125 mL
1 tbsp	xylitol or liquid honey	15 mL
	OR	
2 tsp	agave syrup	10 mL
1	nectarine	1
1	pear or apple	1
1	banana	1
1 1/4 cups	strawberries, hulled	300 mL
	Freshly squeezed lemon juice	

1. *Prepare the sauce:* In a saucepan, combine cocoa and 6 tbsp (90 mL) of the milk. Cook over low heat, stirring until melted and smooth. Stir in the natural sugar of your choice. Add more milk if necessary to thin the sauce (it will thicken more upon cooling). Pour into two ramekins and refrigerate for at least 1 hour, until thickened, or for up to 2 days.

2. Meanwhile, cut fruit into small pieces and sprinkle with lemon juice.

3. Just before serving, artfully arrange fruit on a platter. Serve each person a ramekin of chocolate sauce for dipping.

Stuffed Figs

This quickly prepared dessert will bring an exotic touch from the Middle East to your table. You can also enjoy these figs at breakfast, for an energy boost.

Tip

If the figs are too dry, soak them in warm water for a few minutes.

12	dried Smyrna figs	12
24	large walnut halves	24
2 tbsp	agave syrup	25 mL
12	blanched almonds	12

1. Cut figs in half lengthwise. Dip walnuts in agave syrup. Place 2 walnut halves on 12 of the fig halves and cover with remaining fig halves to enclose nuts. Decorate the top with almonds.

Roman Fig Delight

This recipe has been handed down over generations, and Roman shepherds still prepare it at Christmastime. If you wander through the gates of Rome near the Via Appia, you may see herds of sheep peacefully grazing in the rising evening mist. Whenever I see them, I am surprised to see sheep standing almost in the shadow of St. Peter's Basilica.

Tip

We serve these figs to accompany fruitcake.

18	large dried figs	18
¾ cup	ricotta cheese	175 mL
18	blanched almonds, toasted	18

1. In a bowl, cover figs with warm water and let soak for about 15 minutes or until plump. Drain and pat dry.

2. Using a paring knife, dig a pocket in the figs, starting from the bottom. Spoon 2 tsp (10 mL) ricotta cheese into each pocket, then insert an almond. With your fingertips, gently pinch the pocket closed. Arrange on a serving platter.

Spicy Mango Salad

Serves 4

Choose ripe yet firm mangos and avoid those with shriveled skin. The best ones are imported from Brazil or Peru.

◆ ◆ ◆ ◆

Tip

To cut the mango easily, don't peel it. Carve big, thick slices, put them down flat and use a very sharp knife to divide the flesh of each slice into quarters. You will get cubes that break away easily from their skin.

	Juice of 1 orange	
1	vanilla bean	1
1	cinnamon stick, about 3 inches (7.5 cm) long	1
1/2 tsp	ground ginger	2 mL
1/4 tsp	grated cardamom	1 mL
2	large mangos (or 3 medium)	2
	Fruit sorbet	

1. In a small saucepan, combine orange juice, vanilla bean, cinnamon stick, ginger and cardamom. Heat over low heat for 5 minutes. Remove from heat and let cool. Split the vanilla bean in half lengthwise and scrape the seeds into the juice mixture, stirring to disperse. Discard vanilla pods and cinnamon stick.

2. Peel mangos and cut into small cubes. Divide among dessert bowls and sprinkle with spiced orange juice. Serve cold, with a scoop of sorbet.

Exotic Fruit Salad

4	small mangos, peeled and cut into small cubes	4
2	oranges, broken into segments	2
1 ½ cups	lychees, peeled (or one 18 oz/ 530 mL can, drained)	375 mL
½ cup	unsweetened apple juice, preferably from freshly juiced Granny Smith apples	125 mL
½ tsp	mixed spices (ground ginger, cinnamon and cardamom)	2 mL
2 tsp	agave syrup (optional)	10 mL
6	lime slices	6

1. In a large bowl, combine mangos, oranges and lychees. Sprinkle with apple juice and spices. Taste and add agave syrup if the fruit is too tart. Let soak for 1 hour.

2. To serve, arrange fruit in large glass dishes, sprinkle with the juice from the bowl, then decorate with a slice of lime.

Serves 6

The base of this salad is mango, a fruit low in calories but rich in vitamins and antioxidants. Mango trees are majestic, growing up to 130 feet (40 meters) high. Originating in India, today mangos are cultivated mostly in Asia and South America. Our favorite is the mango from Peru, which is juicy and very fragrant.

Variation
You can replace the agave syrup with 1 tbsp (15 mL) liquid honey.

Yogurt Fruit Salad

We never buy sweetened yogurt or fruit yogurt. Instead, we dress up plain yogurt with fresh fruit. When presented in tall glasses, this dessert looks as good as it tastes.

Tip

Peach skin is not always pleasant to eat and often contains pesticides if the fruit is not organic. So we recommend that you remove it.

2	white peaches, peeled and cut into quarters	2
2	kiwifruit, peeled and sliced	2
1 ¼ cups	strawberries, hulled and cut into quarters	300 mL
1 ¼ cups	raspberries	300 mL
	Freshly squeezed juice of 1 orange	
1 cup	plain yogurt	250 mL
4	fresh mint leaves	4

1. In a large bowl, combine peaches, kiwis, strawberries and raspberries. Sprinkle with orange juice. Cover and refrigerate until chilled or for up to 8 hours.

2. To serve, arrange a little fruit salad in the bottom of four tall glasses and sprinkle with a little of the juice from the bowl. Dollop a few spoons of yogurt into each glass. Repeat layers of fruit and yogurt, finishing with fruit. Garnish with mint leaves.

Caramelized Fig Salad

In late fall, figs may still be found in some market stalls, but they are rarely fully ripe. Strangely, they refuse to ripen even when left for several days at room temperature. This delicious salad allows you to enjoy those "stubborn" figs that have firmly decided not to mature.

Tip

Serve this fig salad hot with vanilla ice cream, which will melt softly in the caramel sauce.

	Grated zest of 1 orange	
	Juice of 4 oranges	
1 tbsp	ground cinnamon	15 mL
1 tsp	ground ginger	5 mL
2 tbsp	liquid honey	25 mL
10 to 12	firm purple figs, cut into quarters lengthwise	10 to 12
	Fresh berries	

1. In a saucepan, combine orange juice, cinnamon and ginger. Heat over low heat until steaming. Stir in honey and simmer for 3 minutes.

2. Reserve 8 fig quarters and add the remaining figs to the saucepan. Cook over low heat, stirring occasionally, for 40 minutes or until the figs are very soft and the honey and orange juice are caramelized. (Be careful not to let the sauce stick; remove it from the heat while still liquid.) Transfer to a bowl and let cool.

3. To serve, place 2 uncooked fig quarters in each serving dish, decorate with berries and sprinkle with grated orange zest. Spoon fig sauce over top.

Dried Fruit Salad with Green Tea

We like mixing this fruit salad with oat flakes to create delicious homemade muesli. We generally prepare it on Sunday evening and keep it cool, to use for several days.

Variations

If you don't like green tea, replace it with unsweetened apple, orange or grape juice.

Add a few fresh raspberries or strawberries (if in season) to liven up your salad.

2 cups	hot brewed green tea	500 mL
1 ¼ cups	mixed dried fruit (apricots, prunes, figs and dates), diced	300 mL
⅓ cup	almonds, walnut halves, sesame seeds or sunflower seeds	75 mL

1. In a heatproof bowl, pour hot green tea over fruit. Cover and refrigerate for at least 4 hours, until chilled, or overnight.

2. To serve, spoon into serving dishes and sprinkle with almonds.

Fruit Jars with Muesli

Serves 6

While this recipe is a great dessert, it's also excellent for breakfast: plenty of proteins and vitamins to start a new day.

Variation
You can use any other frozen or fresh fruit for this recipe.

1 lb	frozen or fresh plums, preferably Mirabelle	500 g
1 or 2	sweet apples, peeled and cut into small cubes	1 or 2
1 or 2	sweet pears, peeled and cut into small cubes	1 or 2
1	vanilla bean, split	1
⅓ cup	heavy or whipping (35%) cream	75 mL
1 cup	ricotta cheese	250 mL
1 tbsp	liquid honey	15 mL
2 cups	crunchy muesli cereal	500 mL

1. If using fresh plums, cut into quarters and remove pits. In a saucepan, combine plums, apples, pears and vanilla bean. Cook over medium heat, stirring often, for 15 minutes or until soft. Let cool.

2. In a bowl, whip cream until firm peaks form. Gently fold in ricotta.

3. Spoon the fruit mixture into small serving bowls or tall glasses. Top with the cream mixture and drizzle with honey. Sprinkle with muesli.

Fruit Yogurt
with Agave Syrup

• •

This quick recipe works well as either dessert or a healthy breakfast.

Tip
If you don't have agave syrup, you can use 8 tsp (40 mL) liquid honey instead.

• *Four 1-cup (250 mL) ramekins or other serving dishes*

2 cups	plain yogurt	500 mL
2 tbsp	agave syrup	25 mL
20	large grapes	20
1	crisp apple, peeled and cut into small pieces	1
1	orange, peeled and cut into small pieces	1

1. In a bowl, whisk yogurt and agave syrup until smooth. Divide evenly among ramekins. Top with grapes, apple and orange. Cover and refrigerate until you're ready to serve, up to 12 hours.

Mint Fruit Soup

Fruit soups are very refreshing in the summer. Plums are among the fruits most recommended by nutritionists.

Tip
Add the strawberries at the last minute so they don't over-soften in the juice.

Variation
Substitute ¾ cup (175 mL) unsweetened grape juice for the orange juice.

6	plums, cut in half or quarters if large	6
3	oranges, peeled and separated into segments	6
½	pineapple, peeled and diced	½
	Juice of 3 oranges, strained	
2 cups	strawberries, hulled and cut in half or into quarters if large	500 mL
3	sprigs fresh mint, leaves chopped	3

1. In a large bowl, combine plums, oranges and pineapple. Pour orange juice over top. Cover and refrigerate until chilled or for up to 8 hours.

2. Stir in strawberries and sprinkle with mint before serving.

Fresh Fruit Soup with Champagne

Serves 6		

When I have friends over for dinner, I never seem to do things simply or on a small scale. I sequester myself in my kitchen for several hours in advance, creating one dish after another. But I often leave myself very little time to prepare dessert. Luckily, fruit soup with champagne is not only quick to prepare, but it's guaranteed to impress.

Tip
For this sumptuous little dessert, choose your fruits well: they need to be ripe and sweet.

20	lychees (or one 18 oz/530 mL can, drained)	20
5	oranges	5
3¼ cups	raspberries	800 mL
2 cups	pink champagne, well chilled	500 mL
6	small sprigs fresh mint or lemon verbena	6

1. Peel lychees and cut in half lengthwise, removing the pit. Peel 4 of the oranges and, holding them over a bowl, cut between the membranes to separate into segments, catching the juice. Juice the remaining orange and add to the collected juice.

2. In a large bowl, combine lychees, orange segments and raspberries. Pour orange juice over top. Cover and refrigerate for at least 30 minutes, until chilled, or for up to 1 day.

3. Just before serving, sprinkle fruit with champagne. Serve in glass dishes, garnished with mint sprigs.

Apple Compote with Red Fruits

We prepare this compote to flavor plain yogurt and ricotta cheese. It gives them a pleasant taste and is a good substitute for sugar.

Tip

Prepare this compote in advance and keep it chilled for up to 3 days. You can use extras for the following day's breakfast.

12	large strawberries, hulled and cut in half	12
10	cherries, pitted	10
1	sweet apple, peeled and chopped	1
1	pear, peeled and chopped	1
¾ cup	raspberries	175 mL

1. In a saucepan, combine strawberries, cherries, apple, pear, raspberries and 1 cup (250 mL) water. Cover and cook over medium heat, stirring occasionally, for 20 minutes or until very soft.

2. Mash fruit with a fork, or transfer to a blender and purée for a smoother texture. Strain through a fine-mesh sieve to remove seeds, if desired.

Dried Apricot Compote with Cardamom

Cardamom, a spice originally from India, is frequently used in northern countries to flavor compotes, mulled wine, ice creams and tarts. It has a peppery taste that differs depending on whether the seeds come from green, black or white cardamom.

Tip

This compote looks beautiful served in glass dishes, decorated with a few edible silver or gold leaves.

1 ½ cups	dried apricots	375 mL
4	cardamom pods	4
3 tbsp	slivered almonds	45 mL
1 tbsp	ground ginger	15 mL
1 tsp	ground cinnamon	5 mL

1. In a saucepan, combine apricots and 3 cups (750 mL) water. Cover and let soak for 3 hours.

2. Add cardamom, almonds, ginger, cinnamon and ¼ cup (50 mL) hot water. Cover and cook over low heat, stirring occasionally, for 30 to 35 minutes or until very soft. Discard cardamom pods. Transfer to a bowl and let cool.

3. Cover and refrigerate for at least 3 hours, until chilled, or for up to 5 days. Serve very cold in small dishes.

Ginger Mango Compote

Mangos are delicious as they are, but they also work wonderfully in compotes, tarts, sherbets, ice creams and so on. Their taste combines particularly well with red currants or blueberries.

Tip
We often serve this mango compote with a scoop of blueberry sorbet.

3	mangos, peeled and diced	3
1	vanilla bean, split	1
3 tbsp	ground ginger	45 mL

1. In a saucepan, combine mango, vanilla bean, ginger and $\frac{1}{4}$ cup (50 mL) water. Cover and cook over low heat, stirring occasionally, for 15 minutes or until very soft. Let cool slightly.

2. Transfer to a blender and purée until smooth. Transfer to a bowl, cover and refrigerate for at least 3 hours, until well chilled, or for up to 3 days. Serve very cold.

Roasted Peach Compote with Ground Ginger

Serves 2	

We like eating this compote with ice cream or sorbet, or sprinkled with blackberry or blueberry sauce before serving.

Variation
Substitute apricots, plums or nectarines for the peaches.

- *Preheat oven to 350°F (180°C)*
- *Rimmed baking sheet*

3	ripe peaches, cut in half	3
3 tbsp	ground ginger	15 ml
	Ice cream, whipped cream or other sauce	

1. Place peaches on baking sheet and sprinkle with ginger.
2. Bake in preheated oven for 20 minutes or until roasted and tender.
3. Serve warm with ice cream.

Rhubarb Compote

My grandmother, convinced that rhubarb was a magic plant for good health, served us this compote at least twice a week for as long as the season allowed her to. It is true that rhubarb contains a lot of fiber and vitamin C.

Tips

This recipe goes very well with yogurt or ricotta cheese.

If stevia is available as a sweetener in your area, you can use it in this recipe by dissolving $\frac{1}{8}$ tsp (0.5 mL) stevia extract powder (or the equivalent of 2 tbsp/ 25 mL sugar) in 2 tbsp (25 mL) extra water and adding it to the rhubarb mixture.

$\frac{1}{2}$ cup	finely chopped rhubarb	125 mL
2 tbsp	xylitol or liquid honey OR	25 mL
4 tsp	agave syrup	20 mL

1. In a saucepan, combine rhubarb and $\frac{2}{3}$ cup (150 mL) water. Cover and cook over medium heat, stirring often, for about 10 minutes or until soft. Stir in the natural sugar of your choice.

2. Serve warm or let cool, cover and refrigerate for up to 3 days and serve cold.

Rote Grütze (German Compote)

This is a very simple and absolutely delicious recipe that my friend Helga left me before leaving Paris and returning to Stuttgart to enjoy a retirement that I hope is as lovely as possible. She prepared this for me one day in her charming and tiny studio on the rooftops of Paris. Her Rote Grütze was an unforgettable delight.

Tips

You can use any soft fruit to make Rote Grütze. Choose fruits that are well ripened and of a sweet variety.

Serve with a scoop of sorbet in summer or with cookies in winter.

2½ cups	strawberries or raspberries	625 mL
1⅔ cups	cherries or blueberries	400 mL
1 cup	unsweetened cherry juice or red wine	250 mL
¼ cup	cornstarch	50 mL

1. In a saucepan, combine strawberries, cherries and cherry juice. Cook over low heat, stirring often, for 10 minutes or until fruit is soft.

2. Dilute cornstarch in a little cold water and pour into the saucepan. Cook, stirring, for about 2 minutes or until thickened.

3. Spoon compote into glass dishes, cool them by dipping them in cold water, then cover and refrigerate for at least 1 hour, until chilled, or for up to 1 day.

Compote in Parcels

One day, our Portuguese friends gave us a wonderful bottle of white port, so delicious that we pinched ourselves in amazement each time we helped ourselves to a small glass. Its unique taste gave us the inspiration for this wonderful compote, ready in a few minutes.

• *Preheat oven to 400°F (200°C)*

2 cups	strawberries, hulled	500 mL
1 cup	raspberries	250 mL
1/4 cup	white port	50 mL
	Chopped fresh mint	

1. Cut two large squares of foil or parchment paper. Place half the strawberries and raspberries in the center of each square and sprinkle with port. Fold to make packages, sealing the edges tightly. Place on a baking sheet.

2. Bake in preheated oven for 15 minutes or until liquid is bubbling. The fruit will swell up and cook in the port. Serve hot or warm in slightly opened envelopes, sprinkled with mint.

Pear Delight

This is an adaptation of a recipe from Normandy that my friend Monique gave me.

Tip

If the pears are too tart, add 1 tbsp (15 mL) liquid honey.

Variation

Replace the pears with a variety of apples that are naturally sweet.

- *6-inch (15 cm) tart pan with removable bottom*

3	large sweet pears, peeled and diced	3
	Juice of 1 lime	
	Hazelnut oil	
	Unsweetened whipped cream or ice cream	

1. In a saucepan, combine pears and lime juice. Let stand for 10 minutes.

2. Add 1½ cups (375 mL) water and cook over very low heat for 1 hour and 45 minutes, stirring occasionally, until pears have dissolved and absorbed all the water. (Keep an eye on it; you might have to add a little more water.)

3. Brush tart pan with hazelnut oil. Spread hot pear mixture into pan, pressing down well. Let cool. Cover and refrigerate for about 4 hours, until chilled, or for up to 1 day.

4. Turn out onto a compote dish and serve with whipped cream.

Pears Poached in Grape Juice

Serves 4

You can poach all types of fruit, but fruits that hold together when cooked work best. Served with ricotta cheese or yogurt, they are also an excellent way to liven up breakfast.

Tip

Serve these poached pears very cold with a pear sorbet and a few cookies.

1 cup	unsweetened grape juice	250 mL
2	whole cloves	2
1	cinnamon stick, about 3 inches (7.5 cm) long	1
1	vanilla bean, split	1
4	sweet pears, peeled and cut into quarters	4

1. In a saucepan, bring 2 cups (500 mL) water and grape juice to a boil over high heat. Add cloves, cinnamon stick and vanilla bean. Reduce heat to low and add pears. Cover, leaving lid slightly ajar, and simmer for 15 minutes or until pears are tender.

2. Discard cloves, cinnamon stick and vanilla pod. Transfer pears and liquid to individual glass dishes and refrigerate for at least 2 hours, until chilled, or for up to 3 days.

Pears Belle-Hélène

4	ripe pears, peeled and halved lengthwise	4
1 cup	xylitol	250 mL
	OR	
¾ cup	agave syrup	175 mL
1 tsp	ground cinnamon	5 mL
7 oz	dark (bittersweet) chocolate, chopped	200 g
½ cup	coconut milk	125 mL
4	scoops vanilla ice cream	4
2 tbsp	unsweetened desiccated coconut	25 mL

1. In a saucepan, combine pears, 3 cups (750 mL) water, the natural sugar of your choice and cinnamon. Bring to a boil over medium heat, stirring to dissolve the sugar. Reduce heat and poach for 8 minutes or until pears are tender. Drain well and set pears aside.

2. In a small saucepan, combine chocolate and coconut milk. Melt over low heat, stirring until smooth.

3. Place pears in serving bowls and pour chocolate sauce over top. Serve with a scoop of ice cream and sprinkle with coconut.

Baked Apples with Oranges and Almonds

Serves 4

At the bottom of our garden, there were centuries-old almond trees. I liked them for their magnificent flowers in the spring and their old winding trunks, which had attached themselves to the wall as if they wanted to escape into the wide world. But oh, how bitter their almonds! To use them, we made all sorts of pastries out of them. Here is a very simple recipe that is quick to make.

Tip

This is a pleasant dessert to finish off the evening meal in winter.

- **Preheat oven to 400°F (200°C)**
- **Shallow baking dish, buttered**

4	large sweet apples	4
2	sweet oranges	2
¼ cup	sliced almonds	50 mL

1. Score the skin around each apple in two rings. Squeeze the juice from 1 orange. Cut the remaining orange into 8 slices.

2. Place the orange slices in four piles in the bottom of the prepared dish. Place an apple on each pile. Sprinkle with orange juice and almonds. Bake for 25 to 30 minutes or until apples are tender. Serve warm.

Apples with Pineapple "Bristled Cats"

*We have nine cats —
seven beautiful Maine
Coon cats and two
adorable alley kittens
we found on the
street. They get along
very well, but as soon
as a "four-footed
stranger" — another
cat, for example —
crosses the doorstep,
they bristle like sea
urchins, or like our
apples in this recipe!*

Tip
Choose a very sweet
pineapple and just-ripe
oranges. Keep in mind
that table oranges are
tastier and sweeter than
juicing oranges.

• *Preheat oven to 375°F (190°C)*
• *Shallow baking dish*

1	small pineapple	1
6	large sweet apples, peeled and cored	6
½ cup	freshly squeezed orange juice	125 mL
2 tbsp	pine nuts	25 mL

1. Peel the pineapple and cut crosswise into 8 slices. Place 6 of the slices in the baking dish and place apples on top. Chop the remaining pineapple and stuff into the center of the apples. Sprinkle with orange juice.

2. Bake in preheated oven for 15 minutes, occasionally spooning juice over top. Stick pine nuts into the apples so they stick out like bristles and bake for 15 minutes or until apples are tender and pine nuts are golden. Serve warm.

Cajun-Style Roasted Pineapple Slices

Serves 4

Here is an old Cajun standby. Of course, in New Orleans, they always add a good splash of rum to the orange juice, which we've omitted here because of rum's high sugar content.

Tip

We like to serve roasted pineapple slices with raisin cake.

- *Preheat oven to 375°F (190°C)*
- *Shallow baking dish*

2	small pineapples	2
1/4 cup	freshly squeezed orange juice (approx.)	50 mL
1/2 tsp	mixed spices (ground cloves and cinnamon)	2 mL

1. Peel the pineapple, cut crosswise into slices and place in baking dish. Sprinkle with orange juice and spices.

2. Roast in preheated oven for about 45 minutes or until pineapple is tender and the juice turns brown. Add more orange juice as needed to prevent the pineapple from sticking to the dish.

Sautéed Pineapple Slices

2	small pineapples	2
1 tsp	butter	5 mL
1 tsp	ground ginger	5 mL
	Fresh mint leaves	
	Fruit sorbet	

Serves 4

This recipe comes from friends in Singapore who operate one of the best restaurants in the city. Pineapple, however widely used in Asian cuisine, was originally native to South America. In 1493, Christopher Columbus discovered the fruit in Guadeloupe and brought it back to Europe. From there, pineapple spread quickly — first to the Pacific, in the hands of the English and the Spanish, then to Southeast Asia, Hawaii, Cuba and Florida, to become one of the most consumed fruits in the world today.

Tip

Those who are more adventurous can flambé the pineapple by adding a bit of alcohol to the skillet before sprinkling the pineapple with ginger.

1. Cut pineapples into quarters lengthwise, without removing the skin.

2. In a skillet, melt butter over high heat. Sauté pineapple quarters until golden on all sides. Sprinkle with ginger. Remove from heat.

3. Cut pineapple into slices, separating the fruit from the skin, and discard skin. Garnish with mint leaves and serve immediately with a scoop of sorbet.

Winter Fruit Kebabs

Serves 4

I don't know who first came up with the idea of putting fruit on a skewer and roasting it, but he or she was truly inspired. You can make kebabs with almost any kind of fruit, depending on the season. This recipe will complement your winter menus.

Tip

To heighten the flavor, you can sprinkle these kebabs with ground ginger. Ginger has a pronounced flavor that will make you forget the absence of sugar in many desserts (or the absence of salt in salty dishes).

- *Preheat broiler*
- *Rimmed baking sheet, lined with foil*
- *Eight 6- to 8-inch (15 to 20 cm) skewers, soaked if bamboo*

4	clementines, thickly sliced	4
2	sweet apples, peeled and cut into large cubes	2
2	mangos, peeled and cut into large cubes	2
1	small pineapple, peeled and cut into large cubes	1
	Freshly squeezed clementine or orange juice	

1. Thread clementine, apple, mango and pineapple pieces onto skewers, alternating the varieties. Place on prepared baking sheet.

2. Broil, turning regularly and leaving the oven door open, for 6 minutes or until golden brown. Serve warm, sprinkled with juice.

Barbecue-Grilled Fruits with Yogurt and Strawberry Sauce

Serves 4

Here is a great idea for an occasion when you have invited friends to an outdoor barbecue but forgot to think about dessert. This recipe also works well with other fruits, as long as they are firm enough to withstand grilling.

Tip
Select ripe but firm fruit.

- *Preheat barbecue to medium-high or preheat broiler*
- *Rimmed baking sheet, lined with foil (if using broiler)*
- *Eight 6- to 8-inch (15 to 20 cm) skewers, soaked if bamboo*

2	apples, cut into bite-size cubes	2
2	nectarines, cut into bite-size cubes	2
	Juice of 1 lemon	
2	oranges, peeled and cut into quarters	2
2 cups	strawberries, hulled	500 mL
1 cup	plain yogurt	250 mL
1 tbsp	liquid honey or xylitol (optional)	15 mL

1. In a bowl, sprinkle apples and nectarines with lemon juice so they do not darken.

2. Thread apples, nectarines and oranges onto skewers, alternating the varieties. Place on prepared baking sheet if using broiler.

3. In a large bowl, mash strawberries with a fork. Stir in yogurt and the natural sugar of your choice (if using).

4. Grill or broil skewers, turning regularly, for about 6 minutes or until golden brown. Serve with the strawberry mixture as a dipping sauce.

Mousses, Creams, Soufflés and Puddings

Melon Mousse with Yogurt and Toasted Almonds

1	small melon	1
1 cup	plain yogurt	250 mL
2 tbsp	slivered almonds, toasted	25 mL

Serves 2

This super-simple dessert is ready in just a few minutes. An infinite number of variations are possible by replacing the melon with mangos, any kind of berries and so on.

Tip

You can replace the yogurt with ricotta cheese.

1. Cut the melon in half. Scrape out seeds, then cut off skin. In a blender, purée melon until smooth.

2. Spoon melon purée into glass sundae dishes and top with yogurt. Sprinkle with almonds.

Chocolate Hazelnut Mousse

A recipe with a name like "chocolate mousse" doesn't need even the slightest introduction — we'll all rush to prepare it and eat it no matter what!

Caution

This recipe contains raw egg whites. If you are concerned about the food safety of raw eggs, use pasteurized whole eggs, separated, or 2 egg yolks and ¼ cup (50 mL) pasteurized liquid egg whites.

Tip

If stevia is available as a sweetener in your area, you can use it in this recipe by dissolving a pinch of stevia extract powder (or the equivalent of 1 tbsp/15 mL sugar) in 1 tbsp (15 mL) extra soy milk and adding it to the cocoa mixture.

⅓ cup	unsweetened cocoa powder	75 mL
3 tbsp	soy milk	45 mL
1 tbsp	xylitol or liquid honey OR	15 mL
2 tsp	agave syrup	10 mL
2	eggs, separated	2
2 tbsp	light butter	25 mL
⅓ cup	chopped toasted hazelnuts	75 mL

1. In a small saucepan, whisk together cocoa, milk and the natural sugar of your choice. Cook over low heat until starting to bubble. Whisk in egg yolks, one at a time, and cook, whisking, for about 2 minutes or until thickened. Remove from heat and whisk in butter until melted. Stir in hazelnuts. Let cool.

2. In a bowl, using an electric mixer, beat egg whites until stiff peaks form. Fold one-quarter of the egg whites into the chocolate mixture, then fold in the remaining whites just until blended.

3. Spoon mousse into two dessert bowls and refrigerate for at least 1 hour, until chilled, or for up to 1 day.

Fig Mousse "Kelly"

Kelly was my first cat, a very large wildcat brought home by my uncle, who found her in the nearby forest when she was a tiny kitten, lost and crying for her mother. We needed to bottle-feed her at first, but she quickly became a true gourmet and adored all the desserts my mother used to bake.

This simple, quickly prepared mousse is delicious and very light. Serve it very cold.

• • ◆ • •

Caution
This recipe contains a raw egg white. If you are concerned about the food safety of raw eggs, use ¼ cup (50 mL) pasteurized liquid egg whites.

1 cup	dried figs	250 mL
½ cup	plain yogurt	125 mL
⅓ cup	ricotta cheese	75 mL
1	egg white	1
2 tbsp	toasted sliced almonds	25 mL

1. In a bowl, cover figs with water; cover and let soak overnight.

2. Drain figs and transfer to a small saucepan. Cook over low heat, stirring often, for 30 minutes or until very soft.

3. Transfer figs to a blender, add yogurt and ricotta and purée until smooth. Pour into a bowl.

4. In another bowl, using an electric mixer, beat egg white until stiff peaks form. Fold into the fig mixture.

5. Spoon into small glass dishes and sprinkle with almonds. Cover and refrigerate for at least 1 hour, until chilled, or for up to 1 day.

Rose Bavarois

♦ ♦

Serves 4

This bavarois is really Bavarian cream, flavored with rose petals.

Tip

Serve very cold. This dessert is excellent with cookies or other biscuits. We prepare cookies the size of the ramekins and, to serve, put a cookie on the plate and turn out the bavarois onto the cookie.

• *Four ³⁄₄-cup (175 mL) ramekins*

1	large untreated rose (or 2 small)	1
¹⁄₂ cup	soy milk	125 mL
1	envelope (¹⁄₄ oz/7 g) unflavored gelatin powder	1
¹⁄₄ cup	cold water	50 mL
3	large strawberries, hulled	3
2	egg yolks, beaten	2
1 tbsp	liquid honey or xylitol OR	15 mL
2 tsp	agave syrup	10 mL
1³⁄₄ cups	whipped crème fraîche	425 mL

1. Separate and chop the rose petals, keeping some whole for decoration. In a small saucepan, bring soy milk to a boil over medium heat and add the chopped petals. Remove from heat and let stand until milk is cooled and flavor is infused.

2. In a small bowl, sprinkle gelatin over cold water and let stand for 5 minutes to soften.

3. In a blender, purée strawberries until smooth. Press through a fine-mesh sieve, collecting the juice and discarding solids. Stir juice into the milk mixture.

4. Whisk egg yolks and the natural sugar of your choice into the milk mixture. Return to medium heat. Cook, stirring constantly, for about 5 minutes or until slightly thickened. Remove from heat and stir in gelatin until dissolved. Dip the pan in a bowl filled with ice cubes so the mixture begins to cool and thicken. Stir in whipped crème fraîche.

5. Rinse ramekins with cold water and fill them with the mixture. Cover and refrigerate until chilled and set.

6. To serve, dip the ramekins in warm water and run a knife around the edge. Invert a plate on top of each ramekin, then turn out onto a plate. Decorate with rose petals and serve.

Almond and Orange Cream

Deliciously flavored and very light, this quick little cream made without dairy products is an excellent way to round off a light meal.

Tip

If stevia is available as a sweetener in your area, you can use it in this recipe by dissolving a pinch of stevia extract powder (or the equivalent of 1 tbsp/15 mL sugar) in 1 tbsp (15 mL) extra orange juice and adding it with the cornstarch.

Variation

You can add the grated zest of 1 orange or replace some of the orange juice with lemon juice.

1 cup	freshly squeezed orange juice, divided	250 mL
1 tbsp	cornstarch	15 mL
1 tbsp	xylitol or liquid honey OR	15 mL
2 tsp	agave syrup	10 mL
1 tbsp	ground almonds	15 mL

1. In a small saucepan, whisk together half the orange juice, the cornstarch and the natural sugar of your choice. Stir in almonds. Cook over low heat, stirring constantly, for 5 minutes or until bubbling and thickened.

2. Gradually whisk in the remaining orange juice. Pour into two heatproof serving dishes and serve.

Chocolate Pots de Crème

These little pots of cream are a traditional dessert in France — we find them on the menu in almost every restaurant. Whether they are caramel- or chocolate-flavored, this dessert is always greatly appreciated.

Tip
Prepare these little desserts the evening before you plan to serve them; they taste best when they're chilled overnight.

- *Six 1-cup (250 mL) ramekins*
- *Stovetop-safe roasting pan*

4 cups	milk	1 L
8 oz	semisweet chocolate, chopped	250 g
½ cup	agave syrup	125 mL
8	egg yolks	8
1	egg, beaten	1
	Boiling water	

1. In a saucepan, heat milk over medium heat until steaming. Stir in chocolate and agave syrup. Cook, stirring constantly, until just starting to boil. Remove from heat. Cover and let cool to room temperature. Strain into a bowl.

2. Whisk in egg yolks, one at a time, then the whole egg. Strain into another bowl. Pour into ramekins.

3. Place ramekins in roasting pan and pour in enough boiling water to come halfway up the sides of the ramekins. Place roasting pan over low heat and cook for about 20 minutes or until water is bubbling.

4. Meanwhile, preheat oven to 300°F (150°C).

5. Carefully transfer roasting pan to the oven. Bake, without opening the oven door, for 20 to 30 minutes or until a tester inserted in the center of a ramekin comes out clean. Transfer ramekins to a wire rack and let cool. Cover and refrigerate for at least 4 hours, until chilled, or for up to 1 day.

Banana and Chocolate Cream

This very light cream is made with yogurt and unsweetened cocoa. If you want to lighten it even more, replace the banana with a pear.

Tip

If stevia is available as a sweetener in your area, you can use it in this recipe by dissolving ⅛ tsp (0.5 mL) stevia extract powder (or the equivalent of 2 tbsp/ 25 mL sugar) in 2 tbsp (25 mL) extra water and adding it to the cocoa.

Variation

You can replace the banana with pears, apples or soft fruits. We've even tested this recipe with fresh figs — it's a delight!

- *Preheat oven to 325°F (160°C)*
- *4-cup (1 L) baking dish*

2 tbsp	unsweetened cocoa powder	25 mL
2 tbsp	xylitol or liquid honey, divided OR	25 mL
4 tsp	agave syrup, divided	20 mL
2	eggs	2
1 tbsp	cornstarch	15 mL
½ cup	plain yogurt	125 mL
1	ripe banana, sliced	1

1. In a double boiler, combine cocoa, half of the natural sugar of your choice and 2 tbsp (25 mL) water. Heat over simmering water, stirring constantly, until smooth. Set aside.

2. In a bowl, whisk eggs with the remaining natural sugar, cornstarch and yogurt until creamy.

3. Arrange banana slices in bottom of baking dish and spread yogurt cream over top. Pour chocolate sauce over cream.

4. Bake in preheated oven for 30 to 35 minutes or until a tester inserted in the center comes out clean.

Ricotta and Chocolate Cream

Here's an ultra-light version of chocolate mousse, with fewer calories. It comes to us from our Florentine friends, who served it to us on the hills above Florence, under the hundred-year-old olive trees on a hot summer's day.

Tip

The berries not only make for a pretty decoration but also bring an extra touch of freshness to this light dessert.

	Juice of 2 oranges	
½ cup	xylitol	125 mL
	OR	
6 tbsp	agave syrup	90 mL
3½ oz	unsweetened chocolate, chopped	105 g
1½ cups	ricotta cheese	375 mL
1 cup	berries	250 mL

1. In a small saucepan, combine orange juice and the natural sugar of your choice. Bring to a boil over medium heat. Reduce heat and boil gently for about 10 minutes or until syrupy. Remove from heat and let cool.

2. In a double boiler, over hot but not boiling water, melt chocolate, stirring until smooth. Remove from heat and let cool.

3. Fold the melted chocolate and ricotta into the orange syrup. Spoon into individual serving dishes, cover and refrigerate for at least 2 hours, until chilled, or for up to 1 day. Serve garnished with berries.

Panna Cotta

Serves 4		

Panna cotta is a traditional Italian recipe that you'll find on the menu of every restaurant and tavern in Italy. The best I have eaten was at the Villa Floridana, a luxurious inn run by the Count of Floridana, a penniless but infinitely charming aristocrat. This villa, all in pink, is located on the road from Rome to Naples, almost halfway between the two cities.

Tips

This is a light dessert, but for even fewer calories, use lower-fat crème fraîche.

If stevia is available as a sweetener in your area, you can use it in this recipe by dissolving 1 tsp (5 mL) stevia extract powder (or the equivalent of $\frac{2}{3}$ cup/ 150 mL sugar) in $\frac{2}{3}$ cup (150 mL) milk or water and adding it to the crème fraîche mixture.

2 cups	crème fraîche	500 mL
1	vanilla bean, split	1
$\frac{2}{3}$ cup	xylitol	150 mL
	OR	
$\frac{1}{2}$ cup	agave syrup	125 mL
1	envelope ($\frac{1}{4}$ oz/7 g) unflavored gelatin powder	1
$\frac{1}{4}$ cup	freshly squeezed orange juice	50 mL
2 cups	berries	500 mL
	Raspberry sauce (optional)	

1. In a small saucepan, combine crème fraîche, vanilla bean and the natural sugar of your choice. Heat over low heat, stirring to dissolve sugar. Remove from heat and set aside.

2. In a double boiler, sprinkle gelatin over orange juice and let stand for 5 minutes to soften. Heat over simmering water, stirring constantly, until gelatin is dissolved. Stir into the crème fraîche mixture. Discard vanilla pod and let mixture cool slightly.

3. Pour into individual bowls or custard cups. Cover and refrigerate for at least 2 hours, until chilled, or for up to 2 days.

4. To serve, dip bowls in hot water and run a knife around the edge. Turn out the panna cotta onto serving plates, garnish with berries and top with raspberry sauce (if using).

Low-Fat Soufflé

This soufflé is made with blackberries and apples, two tastes that go well together. It contains very little fat. Quickly prepared, it is the perfect end to a light meal.

Tips

The baking sheet you place the ramekins on has to be hot.

Run a sharp knife around the inside edge of the ramekins before putting them into the oven; this way, they will rise evenly.

If stevia is available as a sweetener in your area, you can use it in this recipe by adding a pinch of stevia extract powder (or the equivalent of 1 tbsp/15 mL sugar) to the egg whites.

- *Preheat oven to 400°F (200°C)*
- *Six ³⁄₄-cup (175 mL) ramekins, buttered*

3 cups	blackberries	750 mL
1	sweet apple, peeled and diced	1
	Juice of 1 orange	
½ tsp	mixed spices (ground cardamom, cinnamon and ginger)	2 mL
3	egg whites	3
1 tbsp	xylitol	15 mL
	OR	
2 tsp	agave syrup	10 mL

1. In a saucepan, combine blackberries, apple and orange juice. Cook over medium heat, stirring occasionally, for about 10 minutes or until very soft. Transfer to a blender and purée until smooth. Add spices and let cool.

2. Place a baking sheet in the oven to preheat.

3. Place 1 tbsp (15 mL) of fruit purée in the bottom of each prepared ramekin. Set the rest aside.

4. In a bowl, using an electric mixer, beat egg whites until stiff peaks form, gradually adding the natural sugar of your choice. Carefully fold in the remaining fruit purée. Spoon into ramekins and use a knife to level off the top.

5. Place ramekins on hot baking sheet. Bake in preheated oven for 10 to 15 minutes or until puffed and set. Serve immediately.

Banana Soufflé

Serves 6

Soufflés have the reputation of being very tricky to prepare. In fact, there's nothing to it — a soufflé can be easy and quick. It is a small light dessert that very pleasantly rounds off an evening meal.

Tips

To make the egg whites rise more easily, keep them in the refrigerator before using and add a pinch of salt.

Don't open the oven while cooking, as the soufflé could fall.

If stevia is available as a sweetener in your area, you can use it in this recipe by dissolving $\frac{1}{8}$ tsp (0.5 mL) stevia extract powder (or the equivalent of 2 tbsp/ 25 mL sugar) in 2 tbsp (25 mL) extra skim milk or soy milk and adding it with the vanilla.

- *Preheat oven to 400°F (200°C)*
- *8-inch (20 cm) soufflé dish, buttered*

1	vanilla bean, split	1
I cup	skim milk or soy milk	250 mL
2 tbsp	xylitol or liquid honey (optional) OR	25 mL
4 tsp	agave syrup (optional)	20 mL
6	ripe bananas, sliced	6
	Juice of 1 lemon	
3 tbsp	light butter, softened, divided	45 mL
2 tbsp	all-purpose flour	25 mL
4	eggs, separated	4

1. Scrape seeds from vanilla bean into milk in a saucepan. Add vanilla pods and the natural sugar of your choice (if using). Bring almost to a boil over medium heat. Remove from heat and let cool slightly. Remove vanilla pods.

2. In a blender, purée bananas and lemon juice until smooth. Set aside.

3. In another saucepan, melt 1 tbsp (15 mL) of the butter over low heat. Sprinkle with flour and cook, stirring, for 1 minute. Gradually whisk in milk mixture. Cook, stirring constantly, for 2 minutes or until slightly thickened. Remove from heat. Whisk in egg yolks, one at a time. Whisk in banana purée and the remaining butter.

4. In a large bowl, using an electric mixer, beat egg whites until stiff peaks form. Fold one-quarter of the egg whites into the banana mixture. Fold banana mixture into the remaining whites, just until blended. Pour into prepared soufflé dish.

5. Bake in preheated oven for 30 minutes (keeping a close watch) or until puffed and a tester inserted in the center comes out clean.

Pear and Raspberry Soufflé

This soufflé is very light and is the perfect ending to any meal. Serve it with small oatmeal cookies for a healthy dessert.

Tip

If stevia is available as a sweetener in your area, you can use it in this recipe by dissolving a pinch of stevia extract powder (or the equivalent of 1 tbsp/15 mL sugar) in 1 tbsp (15 mL) water and adding it to the raspberries.

Variation

You can replace the pears and raspberries with apples and strawberries or any other fruits.

• **Preheat oven to 375°F (190°C)**
• **6-inch (15 cm) soufflé dish, buttered**

3	sweet pears, peeled and diced	3
	Juice of $\frac{1}{2}$ lemon	
1 $\frac{1}{4}$ cups	raspberries	300 mL
1 tbsp	xylitol or liquid honey	15 mL
	OR	
2 tsp	agave syrup	10 mL
4	egg whites	4
2 tsp	ground cinnamon	10 mL

1. In a saucepan, combine pears and lemon juice. Cook over medium heat, stirring often, for 15 minutes or until soft. Transfer to a blender and purée until smooth.

2. In a microwave-safe bowl, combine raspberries and the natural sugar of your choice. Microwave on High for 30 seconds. Mash with a fork and stir into the pear purée.

3. In a bowl, using an electric mixer, beat egg whites until very stiff peaks form. Carefully fold into the fruit purée. Pour into prepared soufflé dish.

4. Bake in preheated oven for 35 minutes or until golden and puffed. Serve immediately, sprinkled with cinnamon.

Chocolate Orange Soufflé

• •

Serves 2

We prepare this light soufflé in small individual glass ramekins, to make them even more appetizing. Success guaranteed for a romantic dinner by the fire!

Tips

Cocoa powder, like chocolate, is tricky to handle. Always dissolve it in a double boiler; never over direct heat. When dissolving it in water or milk, bear in mind that you should achieve the same consistency as you would when melting chocolate.

If stevia is available as a sweetener in your area, you can use it in this recipe by dissolving a pinch of stevia extract powder (or the equivalent of 1 tbsp/15 mL sugar) in 1 tbsp (15 mL) extra orange juice and adding it to the cocoa mixture.

• *Preheat oven to 400°F (200°C)*
• *Two 1-cup (250 mL) ramekins, buttered*

½ cup	unsweetened cocoa powder	125 mL
1 tbsp	xylitol or liquid honey	15 mL
	OR	
2 tsp	agave syrup	10 mL
	Grated zest of 1 orange	
1 cup	freshly squeezed orange juice	250 mL
1 tbsp	light butter, softened, or hazelnut oil	15 mL
2	eggs, separated	2
1 tbsp	unsweetened desiccated coconut	15 mL

1. In a double boiler, combine cocoa, the natural sugar of your choice and orange juice. Heat over simmering water, stirring until smooth. Stir in butter. Remove from heat.

2. Using a wooden spoon, stir egg yolks into cocoa mixture, one at a time. Stir in orange zest.

3. In a bowl, using an electric mixer, beat egg whites until stiff peaks form. Carefully fold into cocoa mixture. Spoon into prepared ramekins and smooth top.

4. Bake in preheated oven for 12 minutes or until puffed and set. Sprinkle with coconut and serve immediately.

Pear and Almond Clafouti

Serves 6		

Clafouti originated in Limousin, France. The classic version is the cherry clafouti, but there are also blackberry, apple and plum clafoutis. The story goes that there are as many clafouti recipes as there are families in Limousin. Here is ours, made with pears and almonds. It can be served hot or cold.

Variation

To enhance the naturally sweet taste of the pears, add 1 tsp (5 mL) stevia, agave syrup or liquid honey to the milk.

- *Preheat oven to 400°F (200°C)*
- *9-inch (23 cm) quiche dish, buttered*

1	vanilla bean, split	1
2 cups	milk	500 mL
2	eggs	2
2	egg yolks	2
½ cup	ground almonds	125 mL
¼ cup	cornstarch	50 mL
Pinch	salt	Pinch
2	large ripe sweet pears, thinly sliced	2
½ cup	sliced almonds	125 mL

1. Scrape seeds from vanilla bean into milk and add pods. Let stand for 30 minutes to infuse flavor. Discard pods.

2. In a bowl, whisk together eggs and egg yolks. Whisk in ground almonds, cornstarch and salt. Gradually whisk in milk, stirring vigorously to prevent lumps.

3. Spread pear slices over the bottom of the prepared dish. Pour in egg mixture and sprinkle with sliced almonds.

4. Bake in preheated oven for 40 minutes or until puffed, golden and set.

Banana Pudding

Serves 6

Quick and easy to make, this pudding makes a great winter snack when other fruits are not in season.

Tip

We serve this pudding sprinkled with lightly toasted sliced almonds.

- *Preheat oven to 350°F (180°C)*
- *13- by 9-inch (33 by 23 cm) glass baking dish, buttered*
- *Large roasting pan*

1	vanilla bean	1
1¾ cups	soy milk, warmed	425 mL
1 lb	whole wheat bread, sliced and crusts removed	500 g
6	bananas, mashed	6
6	eggs, beaten	6
Pinch	grated nutmeg	Pinch
	Boiling water	

1. Scrape seeds from vanilla bean into milk and add pods. Let stand for 30 minutes to infuse flavor. Discard pods.

2. In a shallow dish, pour milk over bread and let soak for 15 minutes. Drain off any excess milk and transfer bread to a bowl.

3. Stir bananas into bread, breaking up bread to combine. Stir in eggs and nutmeg, mixing well. Spread in prepared baking dish and set dish in roasting pan. Pour in enough boiling water to come halfway up the sides of the dish.

4. Bake in preheated oven for about 40 minutes or until a tester inserted in the center comes out clean. Serve warm.

Dried Fruit Pudding

Serves 6

This pudding does not contain flour and can be considered a healthy choice; just don't eat too much of it in the same week!

Tip

To give the pine nuts more taste, toast them in a dry skillet over medium heat for a few minutes before using.

Variation

To flavor this delicious pudding even more, you can soak the oats in freshly squeezed orange juice or mint tea.

• *8-inch (20 cm) round cake pan, buttered*

½ cup	large-flake (old-fashioned) rolled oats	125 mL
¾ cup	raisins	175 mL
2	eggs, separated	2
½ cup	ground almonds	125 mL
1 tsp	mixed spices (ground cinnamon, ginger, nutmeg and cardamom)	5 mL
	Grated zest of 1 orange	
¾ cup	finely chopped pitted dates	175 mL
½ cup	dried figs, finely chopped	125 mL
¼ cup	pine nuts	50 mL
	Unsweetened whipped cream, plain yogurt or ricotta (optional)	

1. In a bowl, cover oats with water. Cover, refrigerate and let soak for a few hours or overnight. Drain any excess liquid.

2. Preheat oven to 350°F (180°C).

3. In a heatproof bowl, cover raisins with hot water and let soak for 15 minutes. Drain and set aside.

4. In a large bowl, whisk egg yolks until frothy. Stir in oats, almonds, spices and orange zest until well blended. Stir in raisins, dates, figs and pine nuts.

5. In another bowl, using an electric mixer, beat egg whites until stiff peaks form. Carefully fold into fruit mixture. Pour into prepared pan and smooth top.

6. Bake for 50 minutes or until a tester inserted in the center comes out clean. Let cool in pan on a wire rack for 10 minutes.

7. Turn out onto a platter and refrigerate for at least 2 hours, until chilled, or for up to 1 day. Serve with whipped cream (if using).

Virginia Pudding with Apples

We adapted this old family recipe from Virginia to make it lighter.

Variation

To make the pudding better yet, you can replace $\frac{1}{4}$ cup (50 mL) of the flour with ground almonds.

* *Preheat oven to 375°F (190°C)*
* *8-inch (20 cm) soufflé dish, buttered*

$\frac{1}{2}$ cup	raisins	125 mL
	Boiling water	
4 tsp	butter	20 ml
8 oz	sweet apples, peeled and sliced (about 2 small)	250 g
Pinch	ground cinnamon	Pinch
$\frac{1}{2}$ cup	butter, softened	125 mL
$\frac{3}{4}$ cup	whole wheat flour	175 mL
2 tsp	baking powder	10 mL
Pinch	salt	Pinch
1 cup	milk	250 mL

1. In a heatproof bowl, cover raisins with boiling water. Drain and set aside.

2. In a skillet, melt 4 tsp (20 mL) butter over medium-high heat. Add apples and brown on both sides. Remove from heat and stir in raisins and cinnamon. Set aside.

3. In a large bowl, using a wooden spoon, combine $\frac{1}{2}$ cup (125 mL) butter, flour, baking powder and salt. Gradually stir in milk until smooth. Pour into prepared soufflé dish and place the apple slices in the center on top.

4. Bake in preheated oven for 30 minutes or until puffed and a tester inserted in the center comes out clean.

Light Quinoa Pudding with Apricots and Ginger

Ginger goes very well with dried apricots. This pudding, which is delicious for breakfast, has more vitamins and protein than the classic rice pudding.

Variation

If you want to eat this pudding as a snack instead of for breakfast, replace the soy milk with freshly squeezed orange juice. You can also replace the apricots with raisins or dried figs.

²⁄₃ cup	quinoa	150 mL
1 cup	soy milk	250 mL
8	dried apricots, cut in half	8
Pinch	ground ginger	Pinch

1. In a saucepan, bring quinoa, soy milk and apricots to a boil over medium heat. Stir in ginger. Reduce heat and simmer for about 15 minutes or until quinoa seeds burst. Serve immediately.

Bread-and-Butter Pudding with Pecans

This pudding is an English country classic. We prepare it with whole wheat bread, and skim milk instead of cream. We also add orange zest, ground ginger and pecans to make it more succulent.

Tip
Serve hot or warm, lightly sprinkled with agave syrup, if desired.

• *6-inch (15 cm) soufflé dish, buttered*

⅓ cup	mixed dried fruit (such as figs, dates and raisins)	75 mL
4 tsp	light butter, softened	20 mL
6	slices whole wheat bread, crusts removed	6
½ tsp	mixed spices (ground ginger and cinnamon)	2 mL
3	eggs	3
2 cups	milk	500 mL
½ cup	roughly chopped lightly toasted pecans	125 mL
	Grated zest of 1 orange	

1. In a bowl, cover dried fruit with warm water and let soak for 15 minutes or until softened. Drain and dice figs and dates; set aside.

2. Spread butter over one side of each bread slice and sprinkle with spices. Cut into small squares or triangles.

3. Arrange one-third of the bread, buttered side down, over the bottom of the prepared soufflé dish. Place half the dried fruit on top. Layer with half the remaining bread, buttered side up. Add another layer of dried fruit. Finish with a layer of bread, buttered side up.

4. In a bowl, whisk together eggs and milk. Pour over bread mixture. Sprinkle with pecans and orange zest. Cover, refrigerate and let soak for 1 to 2 hours.

5. Meanwhile, preheat oven to 350°F (180°C).

6. Uncover and bake for 45 minutes or until golden brown and a tester inserted in the center comes out clean.

Frozen Desserts

Vanilla Ice Cream with Pecans

Pecans are nuts from a tree that grows primarily in North America, but also in Brazil, Peru and South Africa. Pecans are featured in many North American desserts.

1 cup	table (18%) cream	250 mL
2 tbsp	soy milk or skim milk	25 mL
1	vanilla bean, split	1
3	egg yolks	3
¼ cup	liquid honey, divided OR	50 mL
3 tbsp	agave syrup, divided	45 ml
1 cup	chopped pecans	250 mL

1. In a saucepan, combine cream and soy milk. Bring to a boil over medium heat. Remove from heat and add vanilla bean. Let stand for 30 minutes, then squeeze seeds from vanilla pods into cream mixture and discard pods.

2. In another saucepan, whisk together egg yolks and half the natural sugar of your choice. Gradually whisk in the cream mixture. Place over low heat and cook, stirring constantly, until slightly thickened (do not let boil). Transfer to a shallow, freezer-safe container and let cool.

3. Meanwhile, in a small saucepan, combine pecans and the remaining natural sugar. Cook over medium heat, stirring constantly, for about 3 minutes or until toasted and fragrant. Let cool.

4. Freeze cream mixture, uncovered, for 40 to 60 minutes or until partially firm. Using a fork, break up ice crystals and return to the freezer for 40 minutes. Repeat this process two more times, then thoroughly mix in the pecans and freeze for 1 hour or until firm. (Or freeze in an ice cream maker according to manufacturer's instructions, adding pecans when ice cream is almost frozen.)

Vanilla and Fig Ice Cream

The inspiration for this recipe comes from traditional Italian ice cream. When I lived in Rome, I frequented an excellent gelateria at the bottom of the Spanish Steps, which sold the best fig ice cream in the entire city. I would buy one of these delights and then climb to the top of the Spanish Steps to watch the colorful crowd peering into the fashionable shop windows on Via dei Condotti. I've never dared to ask for the exact recipe, so we improvised our own using dried figs and adding a touch of vanilla.

Variation

You can replace the dried figs with dried apricots or prunes.

¾ cup	coconut milk or soy milk	175 mL
1	vanilla bean, split	1
2¼ cups	dried figs, diced	550 mL
1 cup	table (18%) cream	250 mL
¾ cup	water	175 mL

1. In a saucepan, heat coconut milk over medium heat until steaming. Remove from heat and add vanilla bean. Let stand for 30 minutes, then squeeze seeds from vanilla pods into coconut milk and discard pods.

2. In a blender, purée coconut milk mixture, figs, cream and water until smooth.

3. Pour into a shallow, freezer-safe container and freeze, uncovered, for 2 hours. Using a fork, break up ice crystals and return to the freezer. Repeat this process every 30 minutes for 2 hours or until firm. (Or freeze in an ice cream maker according to manufacturer's instructions.)

Chocolate Ice Cream

1	egg	1
1 cup	soy milk or skim milk	250 mL
¼ cup	xylitol or liquid honey	50 mL
½ cup	unsweetened cocoa powder	125 mL
2 cups	table (18%) cream	500 mL

Serves 4

Xylitol is one of the sugar substitutes most recommended by nutritionists. Most often used in Nordic countries, it is extracted from birch bark and can help prevent health problems linked to excess sugar consumption. Xylitol has the same sweetening power and flavor as conventional sugar but close to half the calories.

Tips
Use a high-quality cocoa powder.

If you like, you can decorate the ice cream with a few mint leaves just before serving.

Variation
For an even creamier cold dessert, add 2 tbsp (25 mL) mascarpone cheese.

1. In a bowl, using a fork, beat egg until frothy. Add soy milk and the natural sugar of your choice. Pour into a small saucepan and cook over low heat, stirring constantly, for about 10 minutes or until slightly thickened (do not let boil). Remove from heat.

2. Whisk in cocoa until blended. Let cool for 15 minutes, then whisk in cream.

3. Pour into a shallow, freezer-safe container and freeze, uncovered, for 1 hour. Using a fork, break up ice crystals and return to the freezer. Repeat this process every hour for 3 hours or until firm. (Or freeze in an ice cream maker according to manufacturer's instructions.)

4. Before serving, transfer to the refrigerator for 30 minutes to soften.

Coffee Ice Cream

To make a good coffee, the red berries have to be picked one by one, by hand. The roasting is also of great importance: to achieve good quality, the beans have to be heated evenly and slowly. In short, freshly ground coffee is the best, as humidity changes its taste.

Caution

This recipe contains raw egg yolks. If the food safety of raw eggs is a concern for you, substitute pasteurized egg yolks or ¾ cup (175 mL) pasteurized liquid whole egg.

Tips

To rev up the flavor and enhance the presentation, garnish with a few chocolate-covered coffee beans.

If stevia is available as a sweetener in your area, you can use it in this recipe by dissolving 1 tsp (5 mL) stevia extract powder (or the equivalent of ⅔ cup/150 mL sugar) in ⅔ cup (150 mL) extra coffee or water and adding it to the egg yolk mixture.

6	egg yolks	6
½ cup	strong brewed coffee	125 mL
⅔ cup	xylitol	150 mL
	OR	
½ cup	agave syrup	125 mL
¾ cup	heavy or whipping (35%) cream	175 mL
2 tsp	unsweetened cocoa powder	10 mL
	Additional unsweetened cocoa powder (optional)	

1. In a bowl, whisk together egg yolks, coffee and the natural sugar of your choice until frothy.

2. In a separate bowl, using an electric mixer, whip cream until stiff peaks form. Fold in cocoa. Whisk into coffee mixture.

3. Pour into a shallow, freezer-safe container and freeze, uncovered, for 1 hour. Using a fork, break up ice crystals and return to the freezer. Repeat this process every hour for 3 hours or until firm. (Or freeze in an ice cream maker according to manufacturer's instructions.)

4. Before serving, transfer to the refrigerator for 30 minutes to soften. Sprinkle each serving with cocoa, if desired.

Raspberry and Mascarpone Ice Cream

The mascarpone gives a creamy base that contrasts perfectly with the raspberry sauce and lime juice. Together, they form an absolutely delicious frozen dessert that is a pleasure to present at the table.

Tips

Pour warmed raspberry sauce over the ice cream before serving to further enhance its presentation and taste.

If stevia is available as a sweetener in your area, you can use it in this recipe by dissolving ¼ tsp (1 mL) stevia extract powder (or the equivalent of 3 tbsp/ 45 mL sugar) in 3 tbsp (45 mL) extra water and adding it to the lime mixture.

	Grated zest and juice of 1 lime	
3 tbsp	xylitol or liquid honey OR	45 mL
2 tbsp	agave syrup	25 mL
8 oz	mascarpone cheese	250 g
1½ cups	raspberries	375 mL

1. In a saucepan, combine 2 cups (500 mL) water, lime zest and juice and the natural sugar of your choice. Bring to a boil over high heat, stirring to dissolve sugar, if necessary. Remove from heat and let cool.

2. In a bowl, whip mascarpone until smooth. Gradually whisk into cooled lime mixture.

3. Pour into a shallow, freezer-safe container and freeze, uncovered, for 40 minutes. Using a fork, break up ice crystals and return to the freezer. Repeat this process two more times.

4. Meanwhile, mash all but ¼ cup (50 mL) of the raspberries with a fork. Stir mashed and whole raspberries into partially frozen ice cream, but do not blend entirely. Spoon into freezer-safe sundae dishes and freeze for several hours. (Or freeze in an ice cream maker according to manufacturer's instructions, adding raspberries when ice cream is almost frozen.)

5. Before serving, transfer to the refrigerator for 30 minutes to soften.

Banana Ice Cream with Dried Fruits and Mascarpone

Serves 2

With this recipe, I wanted to recreate the taste of famous Neapolitan ice cream. In general, I don't like rich ice cream, preferring sorbets, but this is my "Proust Madeleine." It reminds me of a shady terrace in Sorrento, perched high on a cliff overlooking the Bay of Naples, with a view of the island of Capri.

Tip

If the mixture freezes too hard, wait a few minutes before putting it in the blender or add a little lukewarm water.

Variation

If you wish, you can add a few drops of rum to enhance the flavor.

2	bananas	2
	Juice of 1 lemon	
4	dried figs, diced	4
2 tbsp	raisins	25 mL
2 tbsp	mascarpone cheese	25 mL

1. Peel bananas and slice into rounds. In a bowl, drizzle bananas with lemon juice so they do not darken.

2. In a saucepan, cover figs with water and bring to a boil over medium heat. Reduce heat to low and simmer, stirring often, for 20 minutes or until very soft. Drain and stir into bananas.

3. Pour into a shallow, freezer-safe container and freeze, uncovered, for 2 hours.

4. Meanwhile, in a bowl, cover raisins with warm water and let soak for 15 minutes. Drain.

5. Transfer the partially frozen banana mixture to a blender and blend until smooth. Add raisins and mascarpone and pulse until blended. (Or freeze in an ice cream maker according to manufacturer's instructions, adding raisins and mascarpone when ice cream is almost frozen.) Serve immediately.

Hazelnut Ice Cream

This ice cream, which is very easy to prepare, provides the base for many desserts: for example, you could add fruit, melted chocolate or a little whipped cream.

Tips

To lighten this ice cream, you can use soy milk instead of milk.

If stevia is available as a sweetener in your area, you can use it in this recipe by dissolving 1½ tsp (7 mL) stevia extract powder (or the equivalent of 1 cup/ 250 mL sugar) in 1 cup (250 mL) extra milk and adding it to the egg yolk mixture.

• **Preheat oven to 400°F (200°C)**

¾ cup	hazelnuts	175 mL
2 cups	milk	500 mL
4	egg yolks	4
1 cup	xylitol	250 mL
	OR	
⅓ cup	stevia	75 mL

1. Spread hazelnuts on a baking sheet and toast in preheated oven for about 5 minutes or until fragrant and skins start to split. Transfer to a clean towel and let cool slightly. Rub with the towel to remove skins.

2. In a blender or food processor, finely grind hazelnuts and transfer to a bowl.

3. In a saucepan, bring milk almost to a boil over medium heat. Pour over hazelnuts and mix well.

4. In the same saucepan, whisk egg yolks with the natural sugar of your choice until frothy. Gradually whisk in hazelnut mixture. Place over medium heat and cook, stirring constantly, for about 5 minutes or until slightly thickened and almost at a simmer.

5. Transfer to a shallow, freezer-safe container and let cool. Freeze, uncovered, for 1 hour. Using a fork, break up ice crystals and return to the freezer. Repeat this process every hour for 3 hours or until firm. (Or freeze in an ice cream maker according to manufacturer's instructions.)

Banana-Berry Split

This dessert allows for many variations: you can substitute different fruits, ice creams and so on. Our version is extra-light, easy to digest and good for your health.

2	bananas	2
8	scoops vanilla ice cream	8
4 tbsp	agave syrup	60 mL
1/2 cup	fresh blackberries	125 mL
1/2 cup	fresh raspberries	125 mL
1/2 cup	chopped pecans	125 mL

1. Cut bananas in half crosswise, then cut each in half lengthwise. Place two pieces in each of four serving dishes.

2. Place two scoops of ice cream between banana halves. Drizzle each with agave syrup and sprinkle with blackberries, raspberries and pecans. Serve immediately.

Vinci Chocolate and Lavender Sundae

The ancient Greeks were the first to discover the virtues of lavender. The Romans, in turn, became so infatuated with the plant that 1 lb (500 g) of lavender flowers cost the equivalent of one month's salary for an agricultural worker. It was the Romans who introduced this plant to the rest of Europe, during their conquests. This recipe is dedicated to Vinci, one of our handsome Maine Coon cats.

Tip
Use the lavender flowers for garnish sparingly, as they are very fragrant.

2 tbsp	dried lavender flowers	25 mL
2 cups	soy or skim milk	500 mL
2	egg yolks	2
1	egg	1
½ cup	unsweetened cocoa powder	125 mL
¼ cup	lavender honey	50 mL

1. In a bowl, combine lavender flowers and milk. Let soak for about 15 minutes or until flavor is infused. Strain milk through a sieve into a saucepan. Reserve the most beautiful flowers for decoration and discard the remainder.

2. In a bowl, whisk together egg yolks and whole egg until blended.

3. Whisk cocoa and honey into milk. Bring almost to a boil over medium heat, stirring constantly. Whisk a little into the eggs, then gradually whisk egg mixture back into saucepan. Cook, stirring constantly, for about 3 minutes or until slightly thickened.

4. Pour into serving bowls and place bowls in a container half-filled with ice water. Set aside to cool.

5. Once cooled, remove bowls from water and garnish with lavender flowers. Freeze until firm, at least 1½ hours.

6. Before serving, transfer to the refrigerator for 30 minutes to soften.

Mascarpone Fruitcake (page 120)

Summer Cherry Charlotte (page 125)

Baked Apples with Oranges and Almonds (page 157)

Chocolate Orange Soufflé (page 176)

Pear and Almond Clafouti (page 177)

Strawberry Frozen Yogurt (page 196), Avocado Sorbet (page 206) and Pineapple Sorbet (page 204)

Sundae with Prunes and Chestnuts

Serves 6

We tested this dessert for the first time on a hot summer day. Naturally sweetened by the prunes, it melts in the mouth and provides an instantaneous sensation of wellbeing.

Variation

If you wish, you can flavor this dessert with a few drops of white port or rum.

1 ¼ cups	prunes	300 mL
1 cup	drained canned roasted chestnuts	250 mL
1 ¾ cups	light ricotta cheese	425 mL
⅔ cup	whipping (35%) cream	150 mL
	Prunes or whole roasted chestnuts	

1. In a small saucepan, combine prunes, chestnuts and ¼ cup (50 mL) water. Cook over low heat, stirring often, for 20 minutes or until soft.

2. Transfer to a blender and purée until smooth. Transfer to a bowl and stir in ricotta cheese.

3. In another bowl, whisk cream until foamy. Whisk into prune mixture and beat until foamy.

4. Using a piping bag, pipe cream into freezer-safe sundae dishes. Decorate the top with a prune or whole chestnut. Freeze for 2 hours or until firm.

Frozen Yogurt

You can quickly prepare
this super-simple and
refreshing dessert
with any summer fruit.
Children find it a fun
way to eat fruit, even
when they do not
generally like to.

Tip
Decorate with fresh fruit
slices, grated lemon zest
or a few mint leaves.

• *Four ³⁄₄-cup (175 mL) ramekins*

2 cups	summer fruits (strawberries, raspberries, blackberries, blueberries, etc.), chopped, if necessary	500 mL
¹⁄₂ cup	plain yogurt	125 mL

1. In a bowl, combine fruit and yogurt. Spoon into ramekins and freeze for 2 hours or until firm.

2. When ready to serve, quickly pass the bottom of the ramekins under cold running water. Turn each over onto a serving plate and tap the back with a wooden spoon to release. The frozen yogurt should slide out easily.

Frozen Yogurt with Bananas and Blueberries

Serves 2		

In the summer, we love to prepare our own frozen yogurt. It is a tasty, light and healthy substitute for ice cream, which is usually high in fat and sugar.

Variations

You can make this dessert with any fruit you like. Try peaches, pineapple, mango and/or raspberries.

If you like, purée more blueberries for a topping to drizzle over the frozen yogurt.

• **Two ³⁄₄-cup (175 mL) ramekins**

½	ripe banana	½
1²⁄₃ cups	blueberries	400 mL
½ cup	plain yogurt	125 mL
2 tbsp	liquid honey (optional)	25 mL

1. In a blender, purée banana and blueberries until smooth. Transfer to a bowl and stir in yogurt and honey (if using). Spoon into ramekins and freeze for 2 hours or until firm.

2. When ready to serve, quickly pass the bottom of the ramekins under cold running water. Turn each over onto a serving plate and tap the back with a wooden spoon. The yogurt should slide out easily.

Strawberry Frozen Yogurt

3 cups	strawberries, hulled	750 mL
1¾ cups	plain yogurt	425 mL
2 tbsp	xylitol or liquid honey	25 mL
	OR	
4 tsp	agave syrup	20 mL
	Additional strawberries	
	Untreated rose petals	

Serves 6

This blend is a summertime variation of homemade yogurt with fruit.

Tip
If stevia is available as a sweetener in your area, you can use it in this recipe by dissolving ⅛ tsp (0.5 mL) stevia extract powder (or the equivalent of 2 tbsp/ 25 mL sugar) in 2 tbsp (25 mL) extra yogurt and adding it to the strawberry mixture.

Variation
You can replace the strawberries with raspberries, gooseberries, blueberries or any other berries.

1. In a blender, purée strawberries until smooth. Add yogurt and the natural sugar of your choice; pulse until evenly blended.

2. Pour into a shallow, freezer-safe container and freeze, uncovered, for 40 minutes. Using a fork, break up ice crystals and return to the freezer for 1 hour or until firm. (Or freeze in an ice cream maker according to manufacturer's instructions.)

3. Transfer to the refrigerator 15 minutes before serving. Serve in glass sundae dishes, garnished with strawberries and rose petals.

Crunch Frozen Yogurt

We just love ice cream treats with a fruit base, a creamy layer in the middle and a dome piled high with toasted nuts. Here is a much healthier — and no less delicious — version with no sugar and far less fat.

Tip

In winter, try replacing the strawberries with 1 cup (250 mL) prunes, soaked in warm water for 30 minutes and drained.

2 cups	hulled strawberries or quartered plums	500 mL
1 cup	plain yogurt	250 mL
2 tsp	liquid honey OR	10 mL
1 ½ tsp	agave syrup	7 mL
1 tbsp	hazelnuts, toasted and coarsely chopped	15 mL
1 tbsp	pine nuts, toasted	15 mL
1 tbsp	sliced almonds, toasted	15 mL

1. In a blender, purée strawberries until smooth. Set aside.

2. In a bowl, combine yogurt with the natural sugar of your choice.

3. Divide strawberries among freezer-safe sundae dishes. Top with yogurt mixture, then sprinkle with hazelnuts, pine nuts and almonds. Freeze for 2 hours or until firm.

4. Before serving, transfer to the refrigerator for 30 minutes to soften.

Cinnamon Basil Green Apple Sorbet

Serves 2

The idea for this sorbet came to me while I was strolling around a market in Paris one summer Sunday. I came across a merchant with an entire stall of basil: anise basil, Thai basil, cinnamon basil and so on. Cinnamon basil, which pairs well with green apples, imparts a surprising and delicious flavor to this sorbet.

Tips

If you can't find cinnamon basil, use regular basil and add a pinch of ground cinnamon to the sorbet.

If stevia is available as a sweetener in your area, you can use it in this recipe by dissolving ⅛ tsp (0.5 mL) stevia extract powder (or the equivalent of 2 tbsp/ 25 mL sugar) in 2 tbsp (25 mL) warm water and adding it with the basil.

2	Granny Smith apples (unpeeled), diced	2
2 to 3	cinnamon basil leaves	2 to 3
2 tbsp	xylitol or liquid honey OR	25 mL
4 tsp	agave syrup	20 mL
	Additional cinnamon basil leaves	

1. Spread apples in a shallow freezer-safe container and freeze for at least 2 hours or until firm.
2. Transfer to a blender and add cinnamon basil to taste and the natural sugar of your choice. Purée until creamy.
3. Serve immediately, garnished with a few cinnamon basil leaves.

Apricot-Orange Sorbet

Try pairing apricots with oranges — their flavors go together very well.

Tips

It is best to use very ripe apricots for this recipe.

If stevia is available as a sweetener in your area, you can use it in this recipe by dissolving $\frac{1}{8}$ tsp (0.5 mL) stevia extract powder (or the equivalent of 2 tbsp/ 25 mL sugar) in 2 tbsp (25 mL) extra orange juice and adding it to the apricot mixture.

1 lb	apricots, halved	500 g
2 cups	freshly squeezed orange juice	500 mL
2 tbsp	xylitol or liquid honey	25 mL
	OR	
4 tsp	agave syrup	20 mL

1. In a blender, purée apricots, orange juice and the natural sugar of your choice until smooth.

2. Pour into a deep, freezer-safe container and freeze, uncovered, for 1 hour. Using a fork, break up ice crystals and return to the freezer. Repeat this process every 30 minutes for 2 hours or until firm. (Or freeze in an ice cream maker according to manufacturer's instructions.)

Mango Sorbet with Cherry Sauce

Sorbet

1 tbsp	liquid honey	15 mL
1	large mango, peeled and diced	1
1/4 cup	freshly squeezed orange juice	50 mL
	Fresh mint leaves	

Cherry Sauce

1 lb	sweet cherries, pitted, divided	500 g
2 tbsp	xylitol or liquid honey OR	25 mL
4 tsp	agave syrup	20 mL
2 tsp	cornstarch	10 mL
	Grated zest of 1 lemon	
1 tbsp	freshly squeezed lemon juice	15 mL
1/2 tsp	ground cinnamon	2 mL

1. *Prepare the sorbet:* In a small saucepan, combine 3/4 cup (175 mL) water and honey. Heat over medium heat until honey is melted and evenly blended. Remove from heat and let cool.

2. In a blender, purée mango and orange juice until smooth. Add honey mixture and blend until combined.

3. Pour into a freezer-safe container and freeze, uncovered, for 40 minutes. Using a fork, break up ice crystals and return to the freezer or purée in the blender. Repeat this process every 40 minutes for 2 hours or until firm. (Or freeze in an ice cream maker according to manufacturer's instructions.)

4. *Prepare the cherry sauce:* Meanwhile, using a juice extractor or blender, juice half the cherries (press through a fine-mesh sieve to extract juice if using a blender). Cut the remaining cherries in half.

Tip

Serve the sauce hot enough that the sorbet just starts to melt when it is served.

5. In a small saucepan, whisk together 2 tbsp (25 mL) of the cherry juice and the natural sugar of your choice. Whisk in cornstarch, then the remaining cherry juice, lemon zest, lemon juice and cinnamon. Stir in halved cherries and cook over low heat, stirring constantly, for about 2 minutes or until sauce thickens but does not become tacky.

6. Scoop cold sorbet into serving dishes, top with hot cherry sauce and decorate with a few mint leaves.

Melons Filled with Sorbet

You'll enjoy this sorbet in the garden on a hot summer's day.

Variation

You can replace the strawberries and raspberries with other soft fruits, such as cherries, blueberries or blackberries.

4	small melons	4
1 lb	strawberries (or 2 cups/500 mL wild strawberries), hulled	500 g
2 cups	raspberries	500 mL
1 tbsp	lavender honey	15 mL
1 tbsp	hot water	15 mL
	Crushed Ice	

1. Cut 3 of the melons in half crosswise and scrape out seeds. Using a melon baller or small ice cream scoop, scoop out flesh to form melon balls. Set melon shells aside. Place melon balls in a freezer-safe container and freeze for 1 hour or until firm.

2. Peel and seed the remaining melon and chop fruit into chunks. In a blender, purée until smooth. In a bowl, gently combine melon purée, strawberries and raspberries. Cover and refrigerate for at least 1 hour or until chilled.

3. In a blender, purée frozen melon balls with honey and hot water until creamy.

4. Fill melon shells with berry salad and top each with a scoop of melon sorbet. Serve on a bed of crushed ice.

Peach and Passion Fruit Sorbet

Serves 2

There are two varieties of passion fruit: yellow, which can be as big as a grapefruit, or dark purple. They taste identical. Passion fruit pairs well with peach and imparts a refined flavor to this sorbet.

Tip
If stevia is available as a sweetener in your area, you can use it in this recipe by dissolving ⅛ tsp (0.5 mL) stevia extract powder (or the equivalent of 2 tbsp/ 25 mL sugar) in 2 tbsp (25 mL) water and adding it to the passion fruit pulp.

Variation
You can substitute pears for the peaches.

3	peaches (or 4 if small), peeled and cut into chunks	3
1 tbsp	freshly squeezed lime juice	15 mL
4	passion fruit	4
2 tbsp	xylitol or liquid honey OR	25 mL
4 tsp	agave syrup	20 mL
	Fresh mint leaves	

1. In a shallow, freezer-safe container, toss peaches with lime juice to preserve their color. Spread out in a single layer and freeze for 2 hours or until firm.

2. Meanwhile, cut passion fruit in half and scoop out the flesh with a spoon. Place pulp in a small saucepan and discard shells. Heat over medium heat for 1 minute to release the juices. Add the natural sugar of your choice, stirring until dissolved. Strain through a fine-mesh sieve to separate the seeds from the juice, discarding seeds.

3. In a blender, purée passion fruit juice and frozen peaches until smooth and creamy. Serve immediately in glass bowls, garnished with fresh mint.

Pineapple Sorbet

We serve this sorbet in large glass bowls, alternating with blueberry or strawberry sorbet to create a pretty, colorful effect. Served with cookies or muffins, this dish is always a big hit!

Tip

If the sorbet is frozen solid, transfer it to the refrigerator about 30 minutes before serving to soften.

1 tbsp	liquid honey	15 mL
2 cups	unsweetened pineapple juice	500 mL
1	pineapple, peeled and cut into small chunks	1

1. In a saucepan, combine 1 cup (250 mL) water and honey. Bring to a boil over medium heat. Remove from heat and let cool.

2. Pour into a deep, freezer-safe container and stir in pineapple juice. Freeze, uncovered, for 30 minutes.

3. Meanwhile, in a blender, purée pineapple chunks until smooth.

4. Remove the juice mixture from the freezer, mix in the pineapple purée and return to the freezer for 1 hour. Using a fork, break up ice crystals and return to the freezer. Freeze for $1\frac{1}{2}$ hours or until firm.

Raspberry Sorbet

1¾ cups	raspberries	425 mL
2 tbsp	xylitol or liquid honey	25 mL
	OR	
4 tsp	agave syrup	20 mL
1 tbsp	hot water	15 mL

Serves 2

This little sorbet, super-simple and quick to prepare, is our favorite. We enjoy it most during the summer, as the finishing touch to a light meal. It is also an excellent choice if you are on a diet.

Tip

If stevia is available as a sweetener in your area, you can use it in this recipe by dissolving ⅛ tsp (0.5 mL) stevia extract powder (or the equivalent of 2 tbsp/ 25 mL sugar) in 2 tbsp (25 mL) extra hot water and adding it to the frozen raspberry purée.

Variation

This sorbet is also excellent made with blueberries, blackberries, black currants or gooseberries. We always keep some berries tucked away in the freezer during the summer, ready to be transformed into refreshing sorbets.

1. Spread raspberries in a single layer in a freezer-safe container and freeze for 2 hours.

2. Just before serving, in a blender, purée frozen raspberries, the natural sugar of your choice and hot water until smooth. Serve immediately.

Avocado Sorbet

Surprising at first glance, this sorbet is nonetheless superb. Select ripe avocados with no brown spots.

Tips

This sorbet is delicious served with mild ricotta cheese, fromage blanc or plain yogurt.

If stevia is available as a sweetener in your area, you can use it in this recipe by adding a pinch of stevia extract powder (or the equivalent of 1 tbsp/15 mL sugar) and 1 tbsp (15 mL) extra water to the saucepan.

1 tbsp	xylitol or liquid honey	15 mL
	OR	
2 tsp	agave syrup	10 mL
2	avocados, diced	2

1. In a small saucepan, bring 3 tbsp (45 mL) water and the natural sugar of your choice to a boil over medium heat. Remove from heat and stir in avocados. Transfer to a blender and purée until smooth.

2. Pour into a freezer-safe container and freeze for 40 minutes. Using a fork, break up ice crystals (or purée in the blender) and return to the freezer. Repeat this process every 40 minutes for 2 to 2½ hours or until firm. (Or freeze in an ice cream maker according to manufacturer's instructions.)

3. Before serving, transfer to the refrigerator for 30 minutes to soften.

Strawberries and Raspberries with Cucumber Sorbet

	Serves 4	

You will enjoy this healthy recipe on hot summer days.

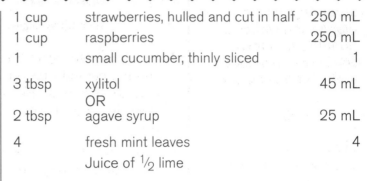

1 cup	strawberries, hulled and cut in half	250 mL
1 cup	raspberries	250 mL
1	small cucumber, thinly sliced	1
3 tbsp	xylitol OR	45 mL
2 tbsp	agave syrup	25 mL
4	fresh mint leaves	4
	Juice of ½ lime	

Sorbet

1 cup	xylitol OR	250 mL
¾ cup	agave syrup	175 mL
Pinch	freshly ground black pepper	Pinch
1	large cucumber, puréed	1

1. In a bowl, combine strawberries, raspberries, cucumber, the natural sugar of your choice, mint leaves and lime juice. Cover and refrigerate until serving.

2. *Prepare the sorbet:* In a saucepan, bring ¾ cup + 2 tbsp (200 mL) water to a boil over medium heat. Add the natural sweetener of your choice and pepper and boil for 5 minutes. Remove from heat and let cool. Stir in puréed cucumber.

3. Pour the cucumber mixture into a freezer-safe container at least 1 inch (2.5 cm) deep and freeze for 40 minutes. Using a fork, break up ice crystals and return to the freezer. Repeat this process every 40 minutes for 2 to 2½ hours or until firm. (Or freeze in an ice cream maker according to manufacturer's instructions.)

4. Scoop sorbet into serving dishes and top with the berry mixture.

Frozen Mango Mousse

Serves 4

Mangos, like any kind of melon, are an excellent choice for those on a diet. They are low in calories and contain many vitamins and antioxidants.

Tip
Try to select mangos from Peru or Brazil, as they are the sweetest.

Variation
You can replace the mangos with 1 large pineapple, weighing about 3 lbs (1.5 kg).

4	very ripe mangos, peeled and chopped	4

1. In a blender, purée mangos until smooth. Press through a sieve into a freezer-safe container, discarding any solids.

2. Freeze for 15 minutes. Using a fork, break up ice crystals and stir to obtain a light-textured mousse; freeze for 15 minutes. Repeat this process every 15 minutes for 1½ hours or until mousse is set.

3. Spoon into individual glasses and serve immediately.

Orange Granita

Serves 4

Granita is a typically Italian granulated sorbet. It's the perfect thirst-quencher for a hot summer day.

Variation
Make seedless watermelon purée in a blender and use it instead of the orange juice. No need to add the honey, as watermelon is sweet enough on its own.

2¾ cups	freshly squeezed orange juice	675 mL
1 tbsp	liquid honey	15 mL

1. In a saucepan, combine orange juice and honey. Bring to a boil over medium heat. Reduce heat and boil gently for 10 minutes. Remove from heat and let cool.

2. Pour into a freezer-safe container, cover and freeze for 40 minutes. Using a fork, break up ice crystals and return to the freezer for 40 minutes. Repeat this process two more times.

3. Before serving, transfer to the refrigerator for 30 minutes to soften.

Grapefruit Granita with Berries

Granita is of Sicilian origin. Perfect for a hot summer day, It Is generally eaten with a straw.

Variation
You can replace the grapefruit juice with orange or mandarin juice.

3 cups	freshly squeezed grapefruit juice	750 mL
1 tsp	grated gingerroot	5 mL
1 cup	xylitol	250 mL
	OR	
¾ cup	agave syrup	175 mL
1 tsp	ground cinnamon	5 mL
2 cups	berries (raspberries, strawberries, etc.)	500 ml
	Fresh mint leaves	

1. In a freezer-safe container, combine grapefruit juice, ginger, the natural sugar of your choice and cinnamon, stirring until sugar is dissolved.

2. Cover and freeze for 15 minutes. Using a fork, break up ice crystals and return to the freezer. Repeat this process every 15 minutes for about 1½ hours or until coarsely frozen.

3. To serve, divide granita equally among glasses and garnish with berries and mint leaves.

Green Tea Ice Cubes

**Makes 2 cups
(500 mL)**

*These ice cubes are
perfect for freshening
and cooling fruit
salads or citrus salads,
bringing the exotic
flavor of a touch of
green tea.*

Tips

If you wish, add a few
fresh mint leaves as the
tea is simmering.

These ice cubes are
equally tasty when made
from jasmine tea.

• *Ice cube trays*

2 tbsp	xylitol or liquid honey	25 mL
2 tsp	loose-leaf green tea	10 mL

1. In a saucepan, bring 2 cups (500 mL) water and
   the natural sugar of your choice to a boil over high
   heat. Add tea, reduce heat and simmer for 4 to
   5 minutes or until well-flavored. Strain out tea
   leaves and let liquid cool.

2. Pour liquid into ice cube trays and freeze for 2 to
   3 hours or until firm.

3. Just before serving, quickly pass the bottom of the
   ice cube trays under hot running water. Place the
   ice cubes in a chilled serving container.

Iced Yogurt Cubes

Serves 4		

Here is a little dessert that is very fresh and healthy — perfect for hot summer days.

• ◆ • •

Tip
You can flavor the cubes with a few finely minced mint leaves.

1 tbsp	unflavored gelatin powder	15 mL
2 tbsp	liquid honey, divided	25 mL
1 tbsp	milk	15 mL
1 cup	plain low-fat yogurt	250 mL
1 cup	raspberries	250 mL
1 cup	red currants	250 mL
1 cup	cherries, pitted	250 mL

1. In a bowl, sprinkle gelatin over $\frac{1}{4}$ cup (50 mL) water and let soften for 5 minutes.

2. In a saucepan, combine 1 tbsp (15 mL) of the honey and milk. Bring to a boil over medium heat. Remove from heat and add gelatin mixture, stirring until gelatin is dissolved.

3. In a bowl, stir yogurt until creamy, then stir into milk mixture. Pour into a dish to a thickness of $\frac{3}{4}$ inch (2 cm) and refrigerate for at least 2 hours or until set.

4. In a clean saucepan, heat the remaining honey over medium heat. Add raspberries, red currants and cherries; cook, stirring gently, for 5 minutes. Let cool.

5. Cut the yogurt gelatin into cubes. Serve on small plates, surrounded with fruit.

Iced Pear Bars

Serves 2

We prepare these bars to set out alongside a pear and chocolate cake. You can flavor them with other fruits, using whatever you have on hand.

Tip

If you don't have an appropriate container to make bars, make ice pops instead. Use plastic juice glasses to make removal easy, and remember to plant a wooden stick in the center when the mixture is half-frozen.

4	ripe pears, peeled and cut into chunks	4
1 cup	unsweetened almond milk or coconut milk	250 mL
2 tbsp	liquid honey or xylitol	15 mL
1 tsp	ground cinnamon	5 mL

1. In a blender, purée pears until smooth. Add almond milk, the natural sugar of your choice and cinnamon; pulse until blended.

2. Pour into a narrow freezer-safe container and freeze for at least 1 hour or until firm.

3. Just before serving, quickly pass the bottom of the container under hot running water. Turn out onto a cutting board and cut into bars.

Coconut Ice Pops

Makes 4 to 6 pops

This fun idea will delight your children. Prepare sorbets of different flavors and colors, then freeze them in ice pop molds with a wooden stick planted in the center.

Tips

When removing the ice pops from the molds, we run them quickly under the faucet and then sprinkle with shredded coconut.

If stevia is available as a sweetener in your area, you can use it in this recipe by adding a pinch of stevia extract powder (or the equivalent of 1 tbsp/15 mL sugar) and 1 tbsp (15 mL) extra soy milk or skim milk to the coconut milk.

Variation

Instead of the coconut milk, soy milk, lime zest and cinnamon, use 2 cups (500 mL) each hulled strawberries and raspberries. Purée with the natural sugar of your choice until smooth and freeze as directed. (This works equally well with other fruits, such as pears, green apples, gooseberries, etc.)

* *Ice pop molds*

1	can (14 oz/400 mL) coconut milk	1
¾ cup	soy milk or skim milk	175 mL
1 tbsp	xylitol	15 mL
	OR	
2 tsp	agave syrup	10 mL
	Grated zest of 1 lime	
Pinch	ground cinnamon	Pinch

1. In a freezer-safe bowl, whisk together coconut milk, soy milk and the natural sugar of your choice. Whisk in lime zest and cinnamon. Freeze, uncovered, for 30 minutes.

2. Using a fork, break up ice crystals and spoon into ice pop molds. Freeze for at least 1 hour or until firm. (If you do not have ice pop molds, use plastic juice glasses and place a wooden stick in the center when the mixture is half-frozen.)

Iced Cappuccino

Serves 4

Cappuccino is, for us, an unmatched gourmet treat, especially the iced cappuccino that we love to stir up during the summertime for an appropriate end to a meal à l'italienne.

Tip
We always serve iced cappuccino with cinnamon and raisin cookies.

2 cups	hot strong brewed espresso	500 mL
5 tsp	xylitol or liquid honey	25 mL
¼ cup	whipping (35%) cream	50 mL
	Unsweetened cocoa powder	

1. In a measuring cup or bowl, combine espresso and the natural sugar of your choice. Let cool.

2. Pour into a freezer-safe container and freeze, uncovered, for 45 minutes. Using a fork, break up ice crystals and return to the freezer for 45 minutes. (Or freeze in an ice cream maker according to manufacturer's instructions.)

3. Before serving, transfer to the refrigerator for 30 minutes to soften.

4. In a bowl, whisk cream until thick. Pour cappuccino into tall serving glasses, add one-quarter of the cream to each and sprinkle with cocoa.

Library and Archives Canada Cataloguing in Publication

Dayan, Ari
    175 natural sugar desserts / Ari and Angelina Dayan.

Includes index.
Translation of: Les desserts sans sucre ajouté.
ISBN 978-0-7788-0228-0

1. Desserts. 2. Sugar-free diet—Recipes. I. Dayan, Angelina II. Title.
III. Title: One hundred seventy-five natural sugar desserts.

TX773.D3913 2009   641.8'6   C2009-902268-0

Index